HAUNTED
JEFFERSON CITY

HAUNTED JEFFERSON CITY

GHOSTS OF MISSOURI'S STATE CAPITOL

JANICE TREMEEAR

Haunted
America

Night scene at the state capitol in Jefferson City, vintage postcard. *Courtesy Janice Tremeear.*

Published by Haunted America
A Division of The History Press
Charleston, SC 29403
www.historypress.net

Copyright © 2012 by Janice Tremeear
All rights reserved

Cover image courtesy of Karen Peterson.

First published 2012

Manufactured in the United States

ISBN 978.1.60949.486.5

Library of Congress CIP data applied for.

CONTENTS

PREFACE

Thanks to Dean Pestana, my soul mate and the love of my life. Not only does he put up with me constantly at the computer researching or writing, but he also goes out with me to gather interviews and take notes and pictures of haunted locations. Thanks also to my kids: Jennifer, who always has room for mom to stay when traveling near the St. Louis area for research or book signings; Nathaniel, who has gotten roped into ghost hunting after tagging along with mom on an investigation; and Charlene, who travels with me riding shotgun and is a part of my paranormal team. Lots of love goes out to my grandchildren, Geoffery, Madison, Tonia, Erica, as well as our newest addition, Sheridan.

Often we utilize dowsing rods to help point us in the correct direction to set our recorders or video or take photos. Many times, our video cameras capture the exact same voice as the recorders. We've recorded on video the misty image of a child darting down the stairs and laughing from a camera set in a hallway on the second floor of an abandoned building. My recorder was near the stairs and also caught her giggle as she darted down—all while the house was totally empty.

As Bess Truman said, "Now about those ghosts. I'm sure they're here and I'm not half so alarmed at meeting up with any of them as I am at having to meet the live nuts I have to see every day."

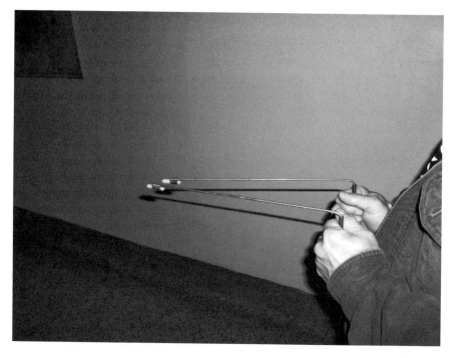

Dean Pestana using dowsing rods at a haunted location. *Photo by Janice Tremeear.*

One cannot begin a quest for the haunted locations without encountering the history of both the locations and the area as well. Some say that these books contain too much history and not enough "scary" ghost stories. I say one often governs the other, for without the history and the events of the past that may have contributed to an imprint or a remaining spirit to be lingering here, there would be no "ghost stories" to tell or research. History gives us an overview of who these individuals were and why those who have passed on might still cling to this earthly plane.

EARLY EXPLORERS

The United States began negotiations in early 1803 to buy the port of New Orleans from France and subsequently wound up with all of the land between the Mississippi and Missouri Rivers' headwaters in what is known as the Louisiana Purchase. Before Meriwether Lewis and William Clark made their famous explorations, early trappers and traders followed the Missouri River. The first Europeans to see the river were the French explorers Louis Jolliet and Father Jacques Marquette, utilizing canoes and dugouts for river travel.

Father Jacques Marquette calling the river "Pekitanoui" (meaning "muddy") in May 1673 led to the misconception of the naming of the river and the state of Missouri. Historically, both river and the state were named after the Siouan Indian tribe, whose Illinois name, Ouemessourita, means "those who have dugout canoes." The grand river has also been called the Big Muddy, Big River, Emasulia sipiwi, Eomitai, Katapan Mene Shoska, Le Missouri, Le Riviere des Missouri, Le Riviere des Osages, Mini Sose, Missoury River, Missures Flu, Mizzou-rye River, Ni-sho-dse, Niutaci, Nudarcha, Old Misery, Pekitanoui, Rio Misuri, River of the West, Riviere de Pekitanoni, Riviere de Saint Philippe and Yellow River.

For several decades, the Missouri River remained unexplored and uncharted until Étienne de Veniard and Sieur de Bourgmont began upstream travel, writing descriptions of the journey in 1713 and 1714. Bourgmont was the first to use the name "Missouri" in reference to the river. He and Étienne de Veniard later established Fort Orleans, the first fort on the Missouri River in 1723, built somewhere near the mouth of the Grand River near Brunswick, Missouri, and named for the Duke of Orléans.

Bourgmont was the first European discoverer of the Platte River, although it is unclear how far on the Missouri River he traveled. The Spanish took over the Missouri River in the 1763 Treaty of Paris, thus ending the French and Indian War; however, they did not extensively explore the river and allowed French fur traders to work along the waterway. Perhaps the most significant expedition before Lewis and Clark was the MacKay and Evans Expedition of 1795–97. James MacKay and John Evans had been hired by the Spanish to search a route to the Pacific Ocean and to alert the British to leave the upper Missouri River area. McKay and Evans created a detailed map of the upper Missouri that was later used by Lewis and Clark.

The Missouri River became the pivot point for all of the major trails opening the American West, including the California, Mormon, Oregon and Santa Fe Trails, as well as the Pony Express at St. Joseph, Missouri. The first bridge built across the mighty Missouri was the Hannibal Bridge in Kansas City in 1869. Paddle steamers soon began moving up the river, helping to facilitate settlement in the Dakotas and Montana. The northernmost navigable point on the Missouri before extensive navigation improvements was at Fort Benton, Montana.

Meriwether Lewis, vintage postcard. *Courtesy Janice Tremeear.*

William Clark, vintage postcard. *Courtesy Janice Tremeear.*

Over the next century, numerous dams, dikes and levees were built along the river for flood control; 35 percent of the river is impounded today. In fact, the only significant stretch of free-flowing waterway today is at the Missouri National Recreational River, a one-hundred-mile National Park that runs between Gavins Point Dam and Ponca State Park, Nebraska, along the Nebraska/South Dakota border. The park is among the last unspoiled stretches of the Missouri River and exhibits the islands, bars, chutes and snags that once characterized the "Mighty Mo." It also preserves the historic ruins of Fort Randall; the Spirit Mound, as well as cultural landmarks important to the Native Americans; and the Meridian Bridge, an engineering marvel of the 1920s.

The majority of Missouri farmers practiced subsistence farming before the Civil War. Those who held slaves had fewer than 5 each. Planters, defined by historians as those holding 20 or more slaves, were concentrated in the counties known as "Little Dixie," in the central part of the state along the Missouri River. Included in the abstract about the farm in Montgomery County where I grew up, located north of the Missouri River, were indications that slaves had once been part of the farm's property. Tensions over slavery in Missouri hinged chiefly on the future of the state and nation. In 1860, enslaved blacks made up less than 10 percent of the state's population of 1,182,012.

INDIANS OF MISSOURI

During the Woodland Period (1000 to 500 BC), the Hopewell tribe inhabited the region now known as Missouri. They learned how to fire clay pots and tools, engaged in trade and created large ceremonial earthworks. They cultivated corn and hunted deer and wild turkey. Missouri was the hunting ground of several tribes, including the Osage, Delaware, Kickapoo, Piankashaw, Sauk and Shawnee tribes in the seventeenth century. However, the Osage Indians occupied the most land in the state, and the river that they settled around would later be named the Osage River. In what is today called Warsaw, Missouri, the Osage Indians lived on the river and settled in the local area in villages. As well as slaves at my childhood home, we often found evidence of Native Americans in the form of pottery shards, arrow and spearheads. Missouri is home to several tales of sightings of Native Americans, long gone, some from the tragedy of the Trail of Tears and others from legends of tribes at war and star-crossed lovers who defied their elders. Often the lands once held sacred to the Indians host strange and unusual occurrences thought to be the results of disrespect shown to the once sacred lands or of the desecration of Native American artifacts and burial places.

A list of the tribes associated with Missouri are as follows: Caddo, Cherokee, Dakota, Delaware, Fox, Illinois, Iowa, Kickapoo, Missouri,

Native American statue, vintage postcard. *Courtesy Janice Tremeear.*

Omaha, Osage, Oto, Sauk and Shawnee. (The Iowas may also be called Ioways. The Ioway Subagency was established in 1825, even though some official contact with the Iowa tribe existed as early as 1822. They were located in the northwestern corner of Missouri in Platte County. In 1829, the Sauks and Foxs of the Missouri were assigned to the Ioway Subagency. Indians under this subagency moved in 1837 to the area near the Great Nemaha River and then were assigned to the Great Nemaha Subagency.)

An Interesting Note for Jefferson City

On the National Register of Historic Places, the Gay Archaeological Site is listed as being in Jefferson City, with address restricted but classified as an Osage City, Aboriginal Historical site. The cultural affiliation is Boone Focus, Late Woodland. The periods of significance are AD 1000–500, AD 1499–1000 and AD 1749–1500.

By the time St. Louis, St. Charles, New Madrid and Cape Girardeau became trading centers, Missouri's Indian history had assumed a definite form. Tall, somber and superstitious, the Osages and the Missouris controlled most of the Missouri country, dividing time between tilling the soil and hunting, and tossing in an occasional war as a diversion. The Missouris lived along the river of that name, with the Osages to the south. An interesting feature of the Osages was the fact that their heads were flat at the back, with protruding foreheads, the result of binding them to boards in infancy.

The fighting Sauks and Foxes moved into northeast Missouri, spreading westward. In alliance with the Ioways, they nearly annihilated the Missouris in 1798. The Potawatomis and the Winnebagoes also stopped for a while in northeast Missouri, and the Kickapoos lived there for a time before migrating southwest. In 1798, Louis Lorimer, founder of Cape Girardeau, married the daughter of a Shawnee chief and brought some of the partly civilized Shawnees and Delawares from Ohio to the vicinity of the cape to act as a "buffer state" between the white settlers and the Osages.

Twenty-one additional Indian tribes, with an aggregate membership of thirty thousand, crossed the Missouri between 1804 and 1825. Some merely traveled through, but others remained for years. Most merely visited the sacred council grounds on the Missouri River near St. Joseph where many tribes came annually at peace for colorful ceremonies and to hear the deliverances of the Prophet through the tribal medicine men.

Peace was promoted by William Clark as Indian agent for the United States and first governor of the Missouri Territory. Hundreds of Indian leaders annually accepted his invitation to visit him in St. Louis for powwows concerning their problems. One massacre did occur, however, long before arrival of the white settlers. The Missouris killed about fifty Spaniards, who invaded their territory in 1720 and brought arms and a plan to incite the Osages against the Missouris. The Spaniards marched into the wrong camp, revealed the plot and distributed the arms, which the Missouris then turned on the invaders. The only attack on St. Louis, on May 26, 1780, ended quickly, with the defenders' cannons terrifying the Indians.

In the beginning of the nineteenth century, Indians in Missouri outnumbered the whites, three to one. As the settlers increased in number, the Indians were driven ever westward. The Sauks and Foxes relinquished their claims in Missouri in 1804, 1815, 1826 and finally (through the Platte Purchase) in 1836, by virtue of which six counties in northwest Missouri were acquired from them and the Iowas. The Osages gave up their lands in the state in treaties signed in 1808 and 1825, moving to Oklahoma, where they still reside. The Shawnees and Delawares departed in 1832, and the Missouris were moved to Oklahoma in 1835.

Many areas report a haunting by Native Americans. Across the state, both private and public locations have ghost sightings ascribed to Indians who once lived in there. Pools and caves are reported to be locations where the spirits of Indians are seen. Waterfalls, rivers and cliff sides from which forlorn lovers have thrown themselves (or been killed by angry fathers) often hold legends of lovers still trying to be with each other in the afterlife. Spook lights in Missouri are often attributed to being the spirits of Native Americans. Locations such as Truman Lake have reports of an Indian chief walking along the road. Big Cedar Hollow in the Ozarks became known as "Devil's Pool" when the White River was dammed to from Table Rock Lake. Indians once lived in the area, and it is said that a "bottomless pit" existed. Legends here say that the ghosts of the Indians haunt the pool. More than one case exists of photographs with images resembling Indians appearing in bonfires, with some described as wearing feathered headdresses, some on horseback and others standing, creating the unnerving feeling of eye contact with the photographer. Is this a mere trick of the dancing flames or a visit from beyond?

Just outside Columbia, Missouri, during a drum circle, I witnessed firsthand dark shapes along the fringes of the woods, shapes that resemble what one would associate with an early Native American. We were in a clearing surrounded by woods, the only lights coming from a clear, starlit sky and the bonfire. Not only were there humanlike figures moving about the woods during the drum circle session, a white misty stag shape also ran from my right to my left in front of me and at the tree line. This was a location where Lewis and Clark had noted cliff paintings of the Great Spirit and was said to have been a meeting place of the tribes, a place scared and meant for peaceful encounters. There were reports of dark, squatty figures dropping from the trees, as well as a malevolent feeling associated with them. Perhaps they were the "little people" of Indian lore that aren't at all like the friendly little elfin folk of the white man. Blasting for the railroad had wiped away the painting of the Great Spirit, and the "little people" of Indian legend are said to be very protective of the land and spirits of nature. At any given point walking the trails within the woods, day or night, one could catch a quick glimpse of something humanlike at the edge of your vision.

Other accounts noted that there were large animal-like beings haunting the woods and some of the outbuildings on the site. In one area I've visited that contains not only the remains of Native Americans but also the terrors brought about by the Civil War, there have been reports of a strange, humanoid creature walking about on all fours with its head rotated backward so the face is turned up toward the sky. This being straight out of a horror movie is strangely pale, almost albino, and lurks within the woods. At this location, while standing on top of the area said to contain the mass graves of Civil War soldiers, I felt what I could only describe as something akin to dozens of scorpions crawling up the back of my head and through my hair.

There were also the sounds of horses all night, complete with saddle and tack, creating the sounds of a rider. A low growl happened at one point to my left side, and I immediately had the impression of a huge mastiff dog growling at me. While walking down the road leading to the site, there was the sound of hoof beats, as if a rider was bearing down on me, ready to run me into the ground, and I instinctively leaped aside as the galloping noise passed. Twice that night I saw a white vision, once as a swirling "dust devil" dancing in the full moonlight and then as a twirling mist moving about between our tents and tiki torches. A car I was sitting in was rocked by unseen hands, and damp handprints were left on the hood. My favorite encounter of the night happened when I turned toward an open field. I had a flashlight on in one hand and wore a headlamp. Both were on, and as I swung about, in the light of my equipment a ghostly white fist came at my face, stopping just short of my left jaw. This happened in what is known as the "Burnt District" of Missouri south of Kansas City, Missouri.

Drumming can also often be heard when no one is drumming. I have been on paranormal investigations with my daughter, who carries an Indian mojo bag. While conducting an electronic voice phenomenon (EVP) session—during which a digital recorder is running to capture frequencies and voice unheard, or sometimes heard, by the investigators—she was talking about her bag. On the playback of the recorder, a distinct sound of beating drums can be heard. We were inside a building with no power or running water of any kind, a few feet from Big River in Missouri and next to a wooded area.

Locations near Columbia, Missouri, report ghosts and that Indian artifacts have been discovered on properties. Most of these appear to have been "protective" and nonthreatening in nature; one private case seemed almost grandfatherly in nature.

All over Missouri are rumors of schools, colleges, hospitals, homes and even resorts being built over not only sacred grounds but also burial sites.

Ghosts of Missouri's State Capital

Missouri's early Native Americans were Mound Builders, and St. Louis was known as Mound City for its abundance of ceremonial mounds. Jefferson City is also said to have Indian mounds in the vicinity; most, as in the case of those at St. Louis, have been destroyed in the course of the white man's progress and building frenzy. Some are unrecognized by the public as Indian mounds, as they simply appear as hillocks covered with trees or brush. Nearly all of the locations built over what are rumored to be Indian sites hold ghost stories. Voices are heard, and objects fly off shelves, sometimes seemingly thrown at people. Drumming, singing and chanting are reported. Sometimes, other tragedies occur such as suicides, rapes, murders and deaths by drowning. State parks once occupied by the Indians often yield sightings. As at the Van Meter State Park, near the Missouri River and west of Jefferson City, a "whoop" was heard, like a warrior might make to his brothers in battle.

Levasy, Missouri, also near the Missouri River and just east of Kansas City, Missouri, has "Bone Hill," where, according to Indian lore, groups of natives stampeded the buffalo and slaughtered them on this hill, leaving the bones to bleach in the sun. The first settlers to arrive in the area found arrowheads, flint scraping tools and bleached buffalo bones in large quantities. Now there are legends of buried treasure (another tale told around the state), as well as a ghost light appearing at the top of the hill, now a cemetery. The light is said to appear once every seven years and is allegedly a farmer coming back to find the gold he buried.

Many people report being visited by the spirits of Native Americans asking to have their remains placed somewhere to prevent people from walking on them. It's said that some people have even heard the sound of Native American drumming coming from the state penitentiary in Jefferson City, Missouri.

As H.G. Wells once said, "New and stirring things are belittled because if they are not belittled, the humiliating question arises, 'Why then are you not taking part in them?'"

MISSOURI RIVER

The river navigation of the West is the most wonderful on the globe, and since the application of steam power to the propulsion of vessels, possesses the essential qualities of open navigation. Speed, distance, cheapness, magnitude of cargoes, are all there, and without the perils of the sea from storms and enemies. The steamboat is the ship of the river, and finds in the Mississippi and its tributaries the simplest theater for the diffusion and display of its power. Wonderful river! Connected with seas by the head and mouth, stretching its arms toward the Atlantic and Pacific, lying in a valley which reaches from the Gulf of Mexico to Hudson's Bay.
—Thomas H. Benton of St. Louis

The artist George Catlin, while sailing as a passenger on the steamboat *Yellowstone*, described the Missouri River as "a huge deformity of waters," and said of it, "There is a terror in its manner."

The *Yellowstone* made its maiden voyage on April 16, 1831, and reached Pierre, South Dakota, on June 19, 1831, six hundred miles farther than any other steamboat, dramatically opening the way for regular travel and trade along the upper stretches of the Missouri River. It returned fully loaded to St. Louis on July 15, 1831. In July 1833, the crew of the *Yellowstone* was overcome by cholera. Many of the crew, including the

Lewis and Clark trail signpost. *Photo by Janice Tremeear.*

firemen, engineer and pilot, died, and the boat was under threat of being burned by locals afraid of contagion. Leaving famed steamboat captain (then a clerk and pilot) Joseph LaBarge to hold and protect the boat and its ailing crew, the *Yellowstone*'s captain, Anson G. Bennett, ventured downstream to St. Louis and soon returned with a new crew. Such was life plying the waters of the Missouri River.

As a tributary of the Mississippi River, the Missouri River at 2,540 miles in length is the longest river in the United States. Important in the explorations and expansion of the American West, the headwaters of the Missouri River are in the Rocky Mountains near Three Forks, Montana, at an elevation of 4,045 feet. The Missouri begins at the confluence of the Jefferson and Madison Rivers and is joined about half a mile downstream by the Gallatin River. It flows from Montana southeast through the Missouri River Basin through North Dakota, South Dakota and Nebraska into Missouri, meeting up with the Mississippi River north of St. Louis. Among the early history-makers to brave this river were Meriwether Lewis and William Clark.

Known as "Old Misery" and "Big Muddy" to early explorers and fur trappers, the Missouri River's treacherous currents and unpredictable moods made the journey up its waters in keelboats heavy with supplies extremely dangerous. Before railroads extended to the Midwest, keelboats, Mackinaws and dugouts carried a steady stream of trappers, traders and adventurers on the river highways. In the very early 1800s, most people said that it was impossible to navigate the Missouri River because of the deadfalls and snags.

In May 1819, the *Independence*, commissioned by Elias Rector and captained by John Nelson, became the first steamboat to successfully navigate the Missouri River, traveling to Franklin in a span of thirteen days (seven days of actual running time). Some reports noted that the extremely challenging trip encompassed fourteen days to traverse nearly two hundred miles from St. Louis to the village of Franklin, Missouri. The steamer left St. Louis on May 15 and arrived in Franklin on May 28. After continuing upriver a short distance to the old town of Chariton (just above present-day Glasgow), the boat returned to St. Louis on June 5. The *Independence* steamed only as far as Chariton, but its trip was deemed a great success. Citizens of Franklin fired cannons in celebration, knowing that the success of the *Independence* meant increased trade for their town. Old Franklin survived only until 1844, when a great flood swept the town away and forced the citizenry to relocate to the present site, located farther from the river and renamed New Franklin.

Next, the SS *Western Engineer*, carrying the military/exploration party of Major Stephen Long, went up the Missouri as far as Council Bluffs. Steamboats docked at Franklin, giving the citizenry another thrill. Designed to terrify the Indians who threatened the expedition, the *Western Engineer* was built to resemble a serpent, with smoke from its boilers issuing from its "mouth."

In 1823, the steamboat *Virginia* was first to navigate the Mississippi from St. Louis to Fort Snelling (Minneapolis). In 1849, the steamboat *White Cloud* was the source of the fire that destroyed twenty-three steamboats and twenty blocks of St. Louis.

Despite the perils of grounding on bars, an ever-changing channel, snags and other obstacles, steamboats continued to push their way up the Missouri. The early steamers were mainly side-wheelers, though a few were stern-wheelers. The preference for side-wheelers continued up to about 1850, but after that date, especially on the Missouri River, the preference switched to stern-wheelers. It is a tradition in the Kinney family of Howard County that Captain Joseph Kinney was one of the main people responsible for influencing the shift to stern-wheel boats on the Missouri River. In terms of numbers, scarcely a dozen steamboats were built by 1817, but in the next two years, more than sixty were launched for traffic on the Mississippi, the Missouri and the Ohio.

The early boats were relatively small, 75 to 150 feet long and 20 to 35 feet wide, characterized by deep, well-rounded, carvel-built hulls with projecting keels and a very marked sheer fore and aft, as well as double-framed hulls housing engines, boilers, a firebox and cargo. A few of the early boats retained their masts and sails. Early engines were low-pressure, condensing, exhaust types that featured walking beams. A single, vertical cylinder was designed to produce maximum piston thrust on the vacuum stroke, but in the late 1810s or early 1820s, high-pressure engines with horizontal cylinders and pitman arms driving counterweighted paddle wheels began to be used. Paired side-wheel engines were introduced in the mid-1820s, and the engine, firebox and boilers were moved to the main deck rather than being in the hold. The Missouri and many other rivers were shallow, demanding design innovations and extremely skillful and observant navigation. Any vessels that plied these rivers had to be designed to move in shallow water and be nimble enough to free themselves from sandbars and other hazards.

Between St. Louis and Kansas City, early Missouri River towns that grew with the steamboat trade were St. Charles, Washington, New Haven, Hermann, Jefferson City, Rocheport, Boonville, Arrow Rock, Glasgow, Waverly, Lexington and Independence.

In 1872, St. Louis ranked second in steamboat traffic, ousted only by New Orleans. In one year (1841), according to St. Louis historian William B. Faherty, St. Louis was reported to have had "186 steamboats land 1,928 times and discharge 263,681 tons of goods."

J.P. Cabanné sent a report as he crossed Missouri by steamboat en route to Council Bluffs: "We are arriving here…3 days and 3 hours since our departure from St. Louis…We are going like an arrow." On their trek westward, Lewis and Clark took two and a half weeks to cover the same distance with keelboats. To a generation that had traveled by pack train or keelboat, downriver, average speeds of up to twenty-one miles an hour were purely unimaginable. Transportation charges were similarly affected. Louis C. Hunter, in *Steamboats on the Western Rivers*, estimated that freight charges between New Orleans and Louisville before the arrival of the steamship were about five dollars per hundredweight. By the mid-1820s, with the introduction of the steamship, freight charges had dropped to as low as 20 cents per hundredweight.

There was, however, a dark side to the speed and ease with which the steamboats were able to travel up and down the river. The ships enhanced the transmission of disease along the river. In 1836, Pierre Choteau Jr. commissioned a third steamboat for the American Fur Company, the SS *St. Peter's*, a 119-ton side-wheeler. This ship would be the transmission vector for one of the worst outbreaks of smallpox among the Indians. The impact and spread of the disease was made far worse by well-meaning whites who attempted primitive inoculations, compounded by ignorance, misunderstanding and poor hygiene. (Some reports include the possessive after the name *Peter* while others do not.) The epidemic might have been limited to a small region had not the ship transported infected individuals far beyond where they could have traveled by foot or horseback. The epidemic ended during the winter of 1837–38, when travel and trade between villages and tribes was greatly restricted. However, by this time, the destruction was nearly complete. It was estimated that the toll was fifteen thousand, but considering the population from which this was taken, it was destruction "almost without parallel in the history of plagues."

Many boomtowns failed to survive through changes in the river's channel. Many died to competition from other towns. One of the earliest settlements no longer extant is Charette, the last location passed by Lewis and Clark on their 1804 expedition. Another was the "town of Missouri," at the "junction of the Missouri and Mississippi Rivers," according to early records. Daniel Boone was one of its early developers.

Not far from St. Charles was Cavern Rock. Near the mouth of the Osage was Formosa. New Baltimore was located a few miles below Dover Landing. Cote sans Dessein, established by the French in 1801, became a thriving town for a time and then faded into obscurity; it was located about half a mile downriver from the mouth of the Osage, on the north side of the Missouri. Nashville, a promising shipping port near Franklin, was swept away by the 1844 flood. Other ghost towns on the lower Missouri were Pinckney Griswold City and Brotherton. Above Old

Franklin were Chariton, Victoria, Grand River City, Doylestown, Carroll City and Alderson. Still others were Miles Point, Caloma, San Francisco, Hill's Landing, Berlin and Mount Vernon.

By 1831, there were five regular packets on the lower Missouri: the *Car of Commerce* (which sank on May 6, 1832), the *Chieftain*, the *Globe*, the *Liberty* and the *Missouri*. Liberty Landing (near the present-day town of Liberty) opened and soon became one of the principal early steamboat ports on the lower river.

By 1860, more than 700 steamboats regularly traveled the Mississippi. The Port of St. Louis logged more than 22,000 steamboat arrivals between 1845 and 1852. Boats lined up for miles next to the city's riverfront. In 1834, there were 230 steamboats on western waters. At the close of 1835, 684 steamboats existed on the western waters (only about 10 were operating on the Missouri River): 304 of these were built in the Pittsburgh district, 221 in the Cincinnati district and 103 in the Louisville district. By 1836, steamboats operating on the lower Missouri River had increased to 15 or 20, making at least 35 round trips to Boonville and Glasgow. In 1838, there were at least 22 boats operating on the lower Missouri River, and the next year, there were at least 39 boats. Between 1840 and 1844, the number of boats operating on the lower Missouri stabilized at about 26, but in 1845, the number of boats jumped to at least 37. By 1849, there were some 58 steamboats operating on the Missouri River.

The real "golden era" of steamboating was the period between 1850 and 1860. By the 1850s, the larger lower Missouri River steamboats and the average Mississippi River steamboats were about 250 feet long, with a 40-foot beam, and carried three hundred to four hundred passengers, as well as some seven hundred tons of freight. A steamboat this size could cost $50,000 to $75,000, but this amount could often be made back in one good season. Sometimes a boat could be paid for in a single trip. During 1858, the peak year for Missouri River steamboating, there existed upward of sixty steam packets and thirty or forty transient or tramp boats operating on the lower Missouri River. In 1859, more vessels left St. Louis for the Missouri River than for both the upper and lower Mississippi. In 1835, the *Missouri Republican* noted, "Every Steamboat that arrives at our wharves is crowded with passengers. Some of the Louisville boats bringing three hundred at a time…many of these remain with us."

Steamboating on the Missouri River became a dangerous proposition due to the roving guerrilla bands that would regularly attack boats below Kansas City. The traffic on the Missouri reached enormous proportions during the war. This increased volume did not originate solely because of the civil conflict. A gold rush in Montana attained its peak in the same period and naturally added names to the passenger lists of the steamboats. For those who traveled the Missouri at this time, it was an exciting and dangerous experience. The outbreak of the Civil War slowed steamboat traffic on the lower Missouri River as most of the boats were used by the Union to transport men and material on the Mississippi. Below Omaha, in the lower river, boats were fired upon by both armies while on the Upper River; they were attacked by Indian tribes, who were becoming bitterly hostile.

After the Civil War, steamboats gliding along on the Missouri River became a common sight. Their design was different than that of earlier steamboats though. These new "mountain boats" were designed specifically for use in Montana's rivers. They had few of the fancy fittings that the boats back east had because light weight was important on the Missouri. They were about 140 to 170 feet long and 30 feet wide. With a shallow hull, "spoon-bill" shaped bow and broad beams, they could carry two hundred tons of cargo though waist-deep water, safely navigating over anything from sandbars to whitewater rapids. In addition, this type of vessel was less expensive to fuel and much easier to steer.

Steamboat crews consisted of three different categories: steamboat mates, firemen and roustabouts. The mates were in charge of making sure that the roustabouts did their jobs. The roustabouts served as the workforce behind the power of a steamboat, often pushing the vessel over sandbars, off snags and through newly formed ice on the river. Firemen had the task of watching for fire on the ship. Boilers in the steam engines often blew up, resulting in devastating fires, especially on earlier steamboats that lacked pressure gauges. The firemen's shifts were mere hours at a time to keep them alert and ready to put a fire out at a moment's notice.

These "mountain boats" meant business. Steamboat captains in the late 1860s could charge as much as $1,200 every month for their services. They had to be extremely skilled captains and good hands at striking bargains with merchants willing to take the risks of sending their goods on the Missouri River for a payoff. The profits of a successful trip from St. Louis to Fort Benton were more than worth it, even considering that the trip took about two to three months. The fare for each passenger was $300; a steamboat could carry cargo worth a profit of up to $40,000, which was a huge amount of money at the time. It is difficult to find details on most of these steamboats.

After the mid-nineteenth century, boats were required to be registered and their boilers certified, but even these requirements documented only such details as name, length, width, depth of hull, sometimes the number of boilers and the diameter of cylinders in the engines and something called "tonnage," which was calculated in different ways at different times. The earlier boats are especially poorly known, partly because the inland river steamboat had to be created to deal with unique conditions on inland rivers, a process that was poorly recorded. Rapid progress involved numerous false steps, hand labor and experiment tempered by experience. Rapid development also took place in building and controlling steam engines to make them more reliable and safe, with the concurrent development of all the associated regulations and legal protections.

The form of the steamboat itself came into being in the 1820s and 1830s. A steamboat is different from the deep-water, deep-draft vessel that has cargo, quarters and everything else set deep in the hull. The new form was simply a long, narrow, shallow pontoon on which cargo was stacked, and cabins were built higher and higher. Some cargo could be placed in the hull, but the engines and boilers sat on the main deck; passengers' cabins and the salon were on the second or "boiler" deck, with perhaps a "Texas" deck above that for the crew; and the pilothouse was perched at the front of the stack for visibility. The hull, much like a bridge, had to be reinforced with an extensive truss system, known as "hog chain" and consisting of long runs of wrought-iron rods over stout "sampson" posts, both along the length, as much as 350 feet, and across the width, up to 40 feet, plus overhanging "guards" that made the main deck even wider than the hull. The wrought-iron rods were fitted with enormous turnbuckles, and by tightening or loosening these turnbuckles, the flexible hull could be "walked" over shallow sandbars.

There were variations in placement of the paddle wheels. Putting them on each side of the hull, as in those boats known as side-wheelers, made for smoother passenger travel and a bit easier steering, but the paddle wheels were outside the lines of the hull, leaving them vulnerable and making the vessel much wider. The stern-wheeler put the paddle wheel at the back, creating a narrower vessel and protecting the fragile paddle wheel by hiding it at the rear of the hull. The stern-wheeler eventually proved more efficient at pushing barges, and it was the stern-wheeler form that survived the loss of the passenger trade brought on by the spread of railroads after the 1870s; in the late nineteenth and early twentieth centuries, stern-wheelers were used for towboats.

The life expectancy of the boats was not long, about eighteen months. Downed trees and other river debris, ice, fire and explosions tended to do in the wooden boats. Some believe that up to 500 wrecked and abandoned steamboats still sit at the bottom of the Mississippi between St. Louis and Cairo, Illinois; 289 documented boats sit at the bottom of the Missouri, but historians believe that during the nineteenth and early twentieth centuries, more than 400 steamboats sank or were stranded between St. Louis, Missouri, and Fort Benton, Montana. To give you some idea of the mortality of steamboats, perhaps as many as 700 different boats operated on the Missouri River between 1819 and the final disappearance of the paddle-wheelers in the first decade after 1900. About 300 of these boats were wrecked during this same period of time. An 1897 report prepared by U.S. Army Corps of Engineers captain H.W. Chittenden, secretary of the Missouri River Commission, gives the names of 273 steamboats wrecked on the Missouri River from the beginning of navigation until 1897. About 100 of these boats were lost in the period between 1820 and 1860.

STEAMBOAT DISASTERS AND HAUNTED STEAMBOATS

A ccording to St. Louis steamboat captain Joseph Brown:

> [F]rom 1840 to 1850 emigration was flowing West. Everything was
> done in a rush, and steamboats multiplied like locusts. They were also
> greatly improved in the manner of construction, size and speed, so that,
> in 1837, there were many large boats running...Owing to the rush of
> emigration at that time, boats could not be built fast enough. It was said
> of a certain boat-yard at Freedom, Pennsylvania that they kept a lot of
> the straight bodies of boats put up. When a man wanted a boat, they took
> him down to the yard and asked him how long he wanted her; then just put
> two ends onto a body and he had a boat. But a really fast and fine boat
> cost about $100,000 to $150,000 and took about eight months to build.

The muddy bottoms of the Missouri and Mississippi Rivers are watery
graveyards to hundreds of sunken steamboats. Some of these magnificent
vessels carry tales of ghost sightings after the deaths of passengers and
crew. Fishermen see spectral beings over the water, misty renditions of
the once grand floating palaces churning upriver or steam pouring from
the smokestacks; there are even eerie tales of severed heads seen floating
in the swirling waters.

Following is a shortlist of steamboats lost to the whims of the river: *Montana, Gordon C. Greene, Bertrand, Kate Swinney, Assiniboine, Saluda, Sultana* and the *Arabia*. Other steamboats to have sunk in the Missouri River are possibly the *Morrow*, a military vessel, and the *North Alabama*, which was headed to Montana and sank on October 27, 1870, near Vermillion, South Dakota, and Obert, Nebraska. The Missouri River at low ebb revealed the wreck of a steamship that sank more than a century ago, as reported on December 4, 2004.

Paranormal activity appears to be strongest in or near rivers. Water is a conductor of psychic energy apparently, as are limestone and electricity (most paranormal investigators love a stormy night). Many ghost tales connected with rivers contain tales of heads floating in the waters, banshee howls along the riverbanks and misty apparitions seen near the site of the disasters.

HAUNTED STEAMBOATS

There are still reports that late at night an invisible boat shoots by the dock, lifting them high with its wake.

—*D.W. Waldron*

Goldenrod

The *Goldenrod* is the oldest riverboat in the nation and the last surviving original Mississippi River Basin showboat in existence. As the last authentic riverboat she was one of the largest and most elaborately decorated showboats ever built and is older than the *Titanic*. The showboat era was a chapter of American history unique to the frontier experience. During the nineteenth century, hundreds of thousands of pioneers lived along the major rivers of the Midwest. The showboat tradition began in the early 1800s. With increased settlement and the advent of new farming techniques, life on the frontier became less overwhelming with regards to time spent on work. Settlers began to look toward the great rivers for new forms of entertainment to fill their days. Showboating quickly became the means of bringing dramatic and musical entertainment to these frontier families. Showboats provided many forms of entertainment, including circuses, minstrel shows and dramas.

Showboating flourished during two distinct periods. The first showboat appeared in 1817. The industry took off with the construction of numerous entertainment vessels, carrying whimsical names such as the *Floating Theatre, Floating Circus Parade, New Sensation, Water Queen, Sunny South* and *Greater New York*. This first period was abruptly cut short with the outbreak of the Civil War. Among other reasons, the great Mississippi River, running north to south and a major thoroughfare for showboats, was cut off by Union troops.

In about 1870, showboating reappeared, and the *Goldenrod* was constructed during this second period. W.R. Markle, considered one of the greatest showboat owners of the era, envisioned building the ultimate showboat. In 1909, Markle's vision became reality, and the *Goldenrod* was built for $75,000 in Parkersburg, West Virginia. It was 200 feet long and 45 feet wide. The exterior was surprisingly sparse, but the interior was the most ornate of showboats. The *Goldenrod*'s interior was modeled after the Majestic Theatre in Denver, Colorado. There were twenty-one theater boxes on two levels, with more than 2,500 lights on the ceiling. Seating capacity reached 1,400. In 1926, this was reduced to 950 seats in order to avoid taxes.

Her ceilings and walls were studded with 2,500 lights clustered in intricate designs. Gilt friezes and highly wrought brass, decorated balcony and box railings. Draperies and upholstery were of red velour, and the floor was richly carpeted. Full-length wall mirrors exaggerated the size of the spacious auditorium. The stage, large and elaborately decorated in frieze and gilt, was well equipped with three drops and eight sets.

To the residents of small communities in the early 1900s, showboats proved to be a rare opportunity for entertainment. These ornate floating theaters and circuses traveled America's inland waterways bringing music and vaudeville acts to audiences onshore. More than fifty showboats traveled the inland waterways of America, braving storms and treacherous currents to make their one-night stands.

Upon completion, the *Goldenrod* embarked on a traveling tour that lasted until 1937. She was permanently docked at the Locus Street landing in the city of St. Louis. At the height of her career, she traveled to over 15 states each season. The showboat traveled as far east as Pittsburgh, west to Omaha and south to New Orleans. As was tradition, the *Goldenrod* did not have her own power and was tugged over the Monogahela, Ohio, Kanawha, Illinois, Wabash, Tennessee and Mississippi Rivers. In 1910, the *Goldenrod*'s tugboat, the *Connie Neville*, sank in a storm. This $21,000 loss was compounded when the *Goldenrod* was blown four miles upstream onto a sandbar.

In 1922, the *Goldenrod* was purchased by Captain Bill Menke. With steam heat for the winter and a cooling system for summer, it played a twelve-month season. The *Goldenrod* received so much publicity as "The World's Greatest Showboat" that the owners did not need to advertise much. A simple announcement of its arrival in the local papers and framed posters set up on the wharf or nearby street were all they needed.

In 1937, the *Goldenrod* docked in St. Louis for a two-week performance. The shows were so well received that it and its cast permanently moored on the levee along the Mississippi River town until 1990. Showboating peaked in about 1910. That year, twenty-one boats traveled the waters of the Mississippi Basin. By 1928, there were only fourteen left and by 1938 only five. In 1964, Frank Pierson purchased and operated the *Goldenrod* until his death in 1990. After many rounds of negotiation, the *Goldenrod* again changed ownership. Dorothy Pierson, widow of the *Goldenrod*'s deceased owner Frank Pierson, began negotiations with the City of St. Charles, Missouri, for sale of the boat. After fifty-three years docked at the St. Louis levee, the *Goldenrod* found a new home on the Missouri River. St. Charles is a medium-sized city located about thirty miles west of St. Louis. This historic town, the first Missouri state capital, is located on the banks of the Missouri River. Famous performers including Bob Hope, Jean Stapleton, Red Skelton, Huntz Hall, Margaret O'Brien and Harry Blackstone all graced the boat's stage.

This beautiful theater boat is said to have been one of the last showboats ever built for the Mississippi River, and it is reported that when Edna Ferber first saw the boat, she fell in love with it, and it inspired her to write her book *Showboat*, on which the musical was based. However, it's likelier that her book was the result of her time spent aboard the *James Adams Floating Theater*.

A ghost reportedly haunts the *Goldenrod*. Many staff members and performers claim that the boat is visited by the spirit of a young girl in a red dress. One of the versions of this story suggests that many years ago, "Victoria," a young girl whose father was a performer on the boat, was brutally murdered along the St. Louis levee. Soon after, the little girl in the red dress began throwing some performances on her own. Staff members and performers claimed to have seen a girl in the red dress on many occasions, and the girl was seen around the boat for many years after. Another version of Victoria's tale suggests that a widower worked on the *Goldenrod* and raised his only daughter on board. Their staterooms were replaced by what would eventually be known as the banquet room. The girl, older in this version, wanted to be a performer on the boat, but her father did not like the idea. Victoria is reputed to have had a stunning figure and a beautiful voice, and although she performed in a few small roles, she never fully realized her dreams of stardom. One night, she and her father had a fight about the subject while docked in St. Louis after Victoria had received several standing ovations and was enjoying her success.

She was hoping to advance from her "bit player" roles, but her father denied her request. Angrily, she left the boat that night to stroll the St. Louis riverfront, a dangerous and deadly choice, as Victoria never returned. Her body was found the next morning floating in the river, her dress shredded and hair tangled about her. There were obvious signs indicating that she'd been beaten. Her killer or killers were never found. The father sank into remorse and began drinking heavily; it's said that heartbreak caused his death shortly after.

Reports of the ghost started after these events, and actors and staff members claim that Victoria is responsible for strange things that happen, such as doors slamming in anger (as if after the fight with her father) and items being moved about and levitated. Some claim to have even seen her roaming about the showboat. She is reported to be seen wearing a red dress with "poofed" Victorian-era sleeves and long, flowing brown hair. Poor Victoria never realized her dreams of becoming a headliner on the *Goldenrod* during her life, but she may still linger in the theater after her death, giving the best performance of her ill-fated career.

Designed in the "steamboat Gothic" style in 1909, the *Goldenrod* showboat was a fixture on the St. Louis riverfront for nearly sixty years.

In 1962, the *Goldenrod* succumbed to fire. The pilothouse, stage roof, wall bracings, stage curtains, scenery, costumes and two staterooms were all lost. Fortunately, the boat was generously restored and renovated. The boat's famous past and careful restoration was honored with a National Landmark designation in 1968. Sadly, it now sits in wasting decay.

City of Saltillo

On May 12, 1910, the huge riverboat *City of Saltillo* sank in the Mississippi River just south of St. Louis and can still be seen in its watery grave. A St. Louisan named Crane was at the helm the boat, which was twice the length of the *Admiral*. He warned passengers that there were dangers lurking in the high water and dense fog. A few hours later, the *City of Saltillo* was helplessly on its side near the bank near Barnhart and Kimmswick, Missouri. Old-fashioned chivalry resulted in the deaths of five women and a baby when the captain ordered them moved to what he thought was a safe place after the *Saltillo* ran into a submerged rock, went into a spin and caught fire. Instead of being a safe haven, the twisting boat threw them all into the dark, turbulent water. All of the cows, pigs and chickens on board were lost. When the water is low, portions of the boat are still visible. The *Saltillo* was traveling to Waterloo, Alabama, to deliver a load of corn, grain and livestock from the St. Louis area.

Gold coins have been discovered at a site located about ten miles west of Mound City, along U.S. 29, on the east shore of the Missouri River near Big Lake. The coins may be from the steamboat *W.R. Caruthers*, which sank nearby. It was carrying $30,000 in gold coins. Examples in

Missouri of paranormal activity near rivers are towns such as Valley Park near St. Louis.

In January 1894, a black resident named John Buckner was taken from the authorities and hanged from the "Old Wagon Bridge" over the Meramec River. The tale following this event claimed that he had sexually assaulted two black women and one white woman in the area. After a crime wave in the county of St. Louis, 150 citizens from the surrounding areas forcibly removed Buckner from the custody of local authorities, dragged him in the middle of the night to the main bridge in Valley Park and lynched him. Valley Park was becoming a boomtown on its way "to rivaling its better known neighbor of St. Louis" until a flood in 1915 pulled the three-span steel bridge down from its foundations. After the electric plants had flooded, nearby businesses burned to the ground and never reopened; 2,000 people found themselves homeless and unemployed, with several victims from the disaster having drowned. Many locals say that a ghost haunts the Meramec River, and some have speculated that the spirit of the lynched John Buckner roams the Meramec where a new bridge (Highway 141) crosses over the spot of the lynching. They say that his ghost longs for revenge on the town and that he is the continuing cause of the bad luck their town has endured.

Builders have removed the skeletal old shacks and rusted railroad trestles that once were the focus of paranormal sightings along Rock Hollow Trail. The true name to the old road is Lawler Road (sometimes Lawler Ford), but it is best known as Zombie Road.

One entrance to the trail is in the 700 block of Ridge Road in Wildwood, with another at the connection with the Al Foster Memorial Trail at the Meramec River near Glencoe. What was once the decaying Lawler Road has been re-created into a beautiful trail for hiking and biking. Rock Hollow serves as an important connector within the Meramec Greenway. This is among the most scenic of Great Rivers Greenway trails and is a wonderful way to connect with nature. Legends that have been passed around for years tell of spectral American Indians. Shawnees are said to have lived in the area, and one family claims that the spirits of these people frequently visited them. Confederate rebels, packs of child ghosts and the tortured souls of working men killed in industrial accidents join the list of ghosts who fell from the cliffs alongside the trail or otherwise met untimely deaths on the road. There are stories of people being run over by trains or asphyxiating in cars left running, as well as those who lived during the speakeasy days of prohibition. There are tales of Della Hamilton McCullough, wife of one of the first settlers in the area, being killed by a railroad car. It is said that her ghost has been seen along Zombie Road.

The first European explorer was French Jesuit priest Jacques Gravier, who traveled the river in 1699–1700. The road likely was built on top of a track used by Indians and early settlers to get to a narrow stretch of the Meramec River. The name "Meramec" is of Algonquian Indian language origin and means "ugly fish" or "catfish," which were abundant in its waters; however, it is possible that the river is named after a band of Miami-Illinois (Inoka) Indians. Early variant spellings of the name were Mearamigoua, Maramig, Mirameg, Meramecsipy, Merramec, Merrimac, Mearmeig and Maramecquisipi. The river early on became an important industrial shipping route, with lead, iron and timber being sent downstream by flatboat and shallow-draft steamboat. Occasionally, the river's name is mistakenly translated to mean "river of death," but this is probably in reference to the number of accidental drownings that occur in it every year. The Meramec has a complicated history and is the site of many tragedies, such as an 1894 lynching, numerous deadly and destructive floods and the site of recent crimes and murders at several Missouri State Parks.

The Meramec connects to the Mississippi River, and the Missouri flows out of the Mississippi. Another river branching off the Meramec (and hence connected to the Missouri) is Big River, where the old Morse Mill Hotel sits empty but for the ghosts freely roaming its halls while the present owner tries to renovate the building.

During the Civil War, it was one of the main routes from western St. Louis County to Jefferson County and was a site of strategic significance. There are tales of Native American spirits haunting the grounds, people who got lost out there, never to return, and drug deals gone wrong. There have been a few accidental deaths out there, along with evidence of strange ritualistic activities that could be cause for some of the

An orb, an example of the reported sightings of strange lights. *Photo by Janice Tremeear.*

paranormal occurrences that are reported. Lawler Road was constructed in the 1860s to provide access to the Meramec River and railroad tracks. It is unknown how the "Lawler" portion of the name came about. It obtained its "Zombie Road" name in the 1950s due to many stories of a local killer named "Zombie" who supposedly lived by the river.

Shadow people, mysterious lights, black masses and orbs have all been reported along Zombie Road

Ghostly Steamboat

At Bonnet's Mill, about seven miles east of Jefferson City, sits a town formerly known as Dauphine. Local legend here notes that if you drive south out of town, you'll find yourself driving before a cemetery and then the road dead-ends at the river. At the junction of the Osage and Missouri Rivers, one can witness a phantom steamboat cruising upriver.

This ghostly-paddle wheeler can also be viewed from the opposite shore from Tebbets. Fishermen along the river here have reported seeing the phantom of a unique steamboat, with a duck-paddle system of propulsion, steaming up the Missouri River. The apparitions of about a dozen passengers can be seen on the deck of the ghost ship, which seems to hover a few feet over the water. These reports come from a location about twenty-seven miles south of Jefferson City.

Delta Queen

The *Delta Queen* and her identical twin, the *Delta King* (known as the "million-dollar boats"), were fabricated from 1924 to 1927 on the River Clyde at the William Denny & Brothers Limited in Dumbarton, Scotland. They were assembled that same year at Banner Island Shipyard in Stockton. The machinery was built by William Denny & Brothers Limited in Dumbarton, Scotland. The paddlewheel shaft and the cranks were forged at Krupp Stahlwerke A.G. in Germany. The boats were completed on May 20, 1927. The *Delta Queen* was put into service on June 1, 1927, starting its career in Northern California, offering overnight accommodations to passengers traveling between Sacramento and San Francisco.

Both steamboats ran for the California Transportation Company of San Francisco on the so-called Delta Route, the Sacramento–San Joaquin River Delta, which gave them their names, taking up regular service on June 1, 1927, and replacing the steamers *Fort Sutter* and *Capital City*. Both boats had their last regular runs on September 29, 1940, the closing day of the Golden Gate International Exposition or World's Fair on Treasure Island.

When World War II began, the *Delta Queen* was commissioned as an auxiliary navy ship. Leased for six months, it was used as floating barracks and a receiving ship for naval reservists, and it also provided ferry service for sailors in the San Francisco Bay area.

The first group arrived on October 16, 1940. The *Delta King* followed in November 1940. However, in April 1941, the navy renewed the leases for another six months. In the fall of 1941, both boats returned to Stockton, but instead of returning them to regular passenger service, the California Transportation Company sold the boats to the Isbrandsten Steamship Company of New York. Both vessels were then towed to the East Coast via the Panama Canal for use as excursion boats on the Hudson River.

Pearl Harbor brought a change in the fate of the boats, rushing both the *Delta Queen* and *Delta King* back into navy service as emergency hospital transports. They were classified July 5, 1944, as Yard House Boats, the *Delta King* as YHB-6 and the *Delta Queen* as YHB-7, but they still retained their names. During the founding conference of the United Nations from April 25 to June 26, 1945, the *Delta Queen* took delegates from the fifty-one gathered nations on sightseeing trips around San Francisco Bay.

In 1946, the boats went into lay-up on Suisan Bay with the Reserve Fleet, called the "mothball fleet." The *Delta King* came off the navy records on April 17, 1946, and the *Delta Queen* on August 28.

On December 17, 1946, after the war, the *Delta Queen* was bought from the War Shipping Administration by Captain Tom R. Greene of Greene Line Steamers of Cincinnati, Ohio, for use on the Mississippi River system. Tom's mother, Mary Becker Greene, was the first person to move aboard the majestic ship. Captain Frederick Way Jr., engineer Charlie Dietz and ship carpenter Bill Horn prepared the *Delta Queen* at Fulton's Shipyard in Antioch, California, for its voyage on sea.

The *Delta Queen* began its legendary voyage through the Panama Canal on April 19, 1947, pulled by the tugboat *Osage*. Arriving in New Orleans on May 18, 1947, after twenty-nine days covering 5,261 miles of open sea, the *Delta Queen* was reassembled and prepared for its voyage up the Mississippi River and the Ohio River to Dravo Corporation on Neville Island, Pittsburgh, Pennsylvania, for a major overhaul. It went back into passenger service on June 21, 1948. Moving from the West Coast to Pittsburgh, it began to cruise the waters of the Ohio and Mississippi and their tributaries.

In 1966, the "Safety of Life at Sea" law nearly ended the *Delta Queen*'s career. Because of its wooden structure, the legislation would end its passenger cruises. With the help of Betty Blake, Bill Muster and E. Jay Quinby, the *Delta Queen* got an extension for two years. Quinby also installed a calliope on the *Delta Queen* that had been rescued from the sunken showboat *Water Queen* and had been made by Thomas J. Nichols as one of the famous "Three Sisters."

By 1969, the ownership had changed to Overseas National Airways. The *Delta Queen*'s extension ran out in November 1970. A "Save the *Delta Queen*" campaign promoted by Betty Blake appeared to fail.

On October 21, 1970, the *Delta Queen* left St. Paul for its final cruise to New Orleans, with Captain Ernest Wagner as master arriving in New Orleans on November 2. On December 31, 1970, President Nixon signed another extension until 1973. Those extensions were prolonged until 2008.

In 1973, the company's name was changed to Delta Queen Steamboat Company, as the Greene family was no longer involved. On April 1976, the *Delta Queen* was sold to the Coca-Cola Bottling Company of New York. After the Prudential Lines Inc. of San Francisco, California, became involved, Sam Zell and Bob Lurie of Chicago acquired control of the outstanding stock in the early 1980s. Then, on October 19, 2001, American Classical Voyages, the parent company of the Delta Queen Steamboat Company (still under control of Sam Zell) filed for Chapter 11. All boats finished their cruises except the *Delta Queen*, which finished the season on January 5, 2002. Fortunately, the Delta Queen Steamboat Company was bought by Delaware North Companies Inc., and the *Delta Queen* went back into service on August 26, 2002, the year of its seventy-fifth birthday.

Another sale of the Delta Queen Steamboat Company happened in 2006, to Ambassadors International, which formed a new cruise line called Majestic America Line. Running beneath its banner were also the *Empress of the North*, the *Columbia Queen*, the *Queen of the West* and other ships.

After the exemption for the *Delta Queen* from the "Safety of Life at Sea" act expired at the end of October 2008, it was no longer allowed to carry overnight passengers. As of February 2009, the *Delta Queen* was located in Chattanooga, Tennessee, and on June 5, 2009, the *Delta Queen* was opened as a floating hotel and restaurant. The *Delta Queen* has eighty-eight cabins on board. It has no televisions, no phones and no internet connections.

The song "Delta Queen Rag" was actually composed by Chattanooga, Tennessee musician Lon Eldridge while sitting on the riverbank by the *Delta Queen*. One of the highlights of its career came when President Jimmy Carter and his family took a cruise in 1979 from St. Paul, Minnesota, to St. Louis, Missouri. For the occasion, the *Delta Queen* proudly bore a sign that read "Steamboat One." Princess Margaret of England and other celebrities have also traveled aboard the great lady, and it is renowned for being a honeymoon destination.

The *Delta Queen* was once a participant in steamboat races, as many did in the past. The most famous was a race from New Orleans to St. Louis in 1870 when the *Robert E. Lee* bested the *Natchez*. Steamboat racing back then was dangerous, as the engine and boiler technology had not kept pace with the egos of the steamboat captains. There were fires and explosions galore. The winning steamboat was generally the one that didn't blow up.

Since 1963, one tradition was the annual Great Steamboat Race, held between the *Belle of Louisville* and the immortal *Delta Queen*. The *Belle of Louisville* dates to 1914 and the *Delta Queen* to 1926, and both were registered National Historic Landmarks, so it was a race without peer. Each was fully steam powered, and each had pride on the line every year when they left the landing at Louisville, Kentucky, for the two-hour sprint as part of the larger Kentucky Derby Festival held in the days before the big horse race. The winner took home the famed Golden Antlers in recognition of its status as the fastest boat on the river. That tradition came to an end in 2008 when the *Delta Queen* was retired to become a floating hotel in Chattanooga.

Guests feel a part of history within the wall of the *Delta Queen*, and that in itself holds a haunting all its own, but indeed there is a ghost reported to stroll the decks and halls of the boat. As the resident ghost of the *Delta Queen*, Mary Becker Greene was the first woman ever licensed to pilot a steamboat in America. Mary Becker married Captain Gordon C. Greene in 1890 and set up housekeeping on the *H.K. Bedford*, his Cincinnati packet boat. As she stood watch with her husband in the pilothouse, she learned the details of steamboat operation and piloting. Greene was granted her pilot's license in 1896, one of the first women ever to achieve this, if not the first. Some stories also note that she was given the nickname of Captain Molly.

She originally took command of the *Argand*, which operated at a good profit. At the time, packet boats were losing business to the expanding railroads, but the Greene Lines were able to show a profit because customers liked the "lady captain's" dependability and refinement. It's said that in an interview Mary declared that seeing a woman in charge of a riverboat was such a novelty that she chose to always take the night duty to avoid being a spectacle.

Tales abound about Mary defeating her husband in a steamboat race in 1903, and when the next year the World's Fair debuted in St. Louis, she was entrusted to pilot Gordon's newest boat, the *Greenland*, to the city for display. In 1946, Captain Tom Greene (who had been on steamboats since his birth) decided to invest the profits in a second passenger vessel. In California, he saved from the ship breakers the luxurious pride of the Sacramento River, the *Delta Queen*.

When Captain Tom had the *Delta Queen* boarded up and towed through the Panama Canal, newspapers from all over the world provided daily updates of the journey. Incredibly, at the end of a month-long journey, the *Delta Queen* was delivered safely to New Orleans. Extensive renovation and refitting followed, and on June 30, 1948, the new flagship of the Greene Lines and its lady captain were ready to welcome the public.

Captain Mary moved aboard the *Delta Queen* after it was purchased by her son, and she spent the last years of her life on it. She lived in Cabin G, which was specially fitted to meet her needs. Ma Greene (as she was sometimes called) played an important role in the establishment of the *Delta Queen*. She was one of the founders of the Delta Queen Steamboat Company. She was was very much "in tune" to the *Delta Queen*, taking special care to ensure that it was a family-friendly place where everyone could enjoy their time. She was also known to hold very strong opinions and, as an avid temperance backer, did not approve of the sale of alcohol on her ship.

A vibrant lady, she captivated passengers with wild tales of river life and even danced with them two days before her death on April 22, 1949, in her cabin after sixty years as master and pilot of some of the finest steamboats on the inland river system. Captain Tom Greene died the following year while at the wheel of the *Delta Queen*.

While several worked to uphold the legacy of Mary B. Greene and adhere to her wishes, a saloon was established onboard the *Delta Queen* shortly after Mary passed. Just after the first cocktail was sold, a barge crashed into the boat, shattering the bar. The crew was shocked and amazed once they uncovered the barge and saw that it had a familiar name: the *Captain Mary B*. This was the start of the strange paranormal events that began to take place with the *Delta Queen*. Did the ghost of Ma Green cause the bar on the *Delta Queen* to be shattered? The crew firmly believed that this experience was Ma Greene expressing her unhappiness with the saloon.

Even now, death can't keep Captain Mary Becker Greene from boarding her beloved *Delta Queen* steamboat. Several guests report encounters with the *Delta Queen*'s resident ghost as she closes doors, turns off lights and keeps watch over the crew.

One of these encounters happened to Captain Mike Williams as he slept aboard the ship one night during its annual refurbishment in 1982. Someone whispered *psst* in his ear, and he felt the person's breath. He didn't get up, and twice more it happened before he checked the room and saw no one. One version to the tale states that Williams, deciding that he better go check the cabins, followed the sound of a slamming door to the engine room, where he discovered water rushing in from a broken pipe from the boilers that was soon repaired.

A second version is much the same, with the exception of Williams checking all the doors until he came to room 109, the room in which Captain Mary Becker Greene died. Then he saw water rushing into the lower level of the boat from a hole in the hull that was quickly repaired. This hole had been big enough to sink the ship if it hadn't been discovered in time. Regardless of the water coming in from a broken pipe or a hole in the hull, repairs were made, and Williams said, "Had I not been awakened, the *Delta Queen* might have been in big trouble."

He also believed that Captain Mary Greene led him to his wife. At the time, Mary Fruge was a new employee on the *Delta Queen*. She received a call from a sick passenger in room 109. She knew nothing of the ghost stories, and she called Captain Williams to go check on the passenger. When he got to the room, no one was there. This encounter led Mary Fruge and Captain Williams to get better acquainted, and they were married less than a year later. "There is something very benevolent and kind, sometimes stern like a great-grandmother," said Captain Williams, who retired three years after this story. "That's the kind of spirit that dwells in this boat."

Throughout history, many individuals have traveled aboard the *Delta Queen*. These individuals include military personnel, guests and crew members. Most of these people will attest to the fact that they still feel as if Captain Mary is aboard her beloved vessel. Many have claimed to have seen an apparition that resembles this lady.

There is the story of a photographer taking souvenir shots of tourist in the saloon. He fell backward, appearing distraught, and people rushed to his aid. "She's alive," he said. "She's alive in the picture frame." Captain Mary's portrait had been in the background for many of the photos, and it had suddenly changed position, according to the photographer. The woman in the frame had switched and was now facing him; she also made other movements within the frame, or so he said. The man was traumatized and is said to have never worked on the boat again.

Another oft-told tale is of a female entertainer (several variations of this story exist) returning to her quarters after most people had retired for the evening. She disliked the eeriness of the long corridor of closed doors and was heartened to see an elderly woman in a green floor-length formal cloak. After turning a certain corner, the woman slipped silently into her room and disappeared without pausing to bring out a key and unlock her door. One night, the green-cloaked woman disappeared in the middle of the corridor in front of the entertainer, and the performer, knowing the tales of the ghost of Mary Greene, took courage form the presence of the spirit.

A few cases show Captain Mary's playfulness. A tour guide claimed to have noticed on several occasions a woman dressed in outmoded clothing. The guide was worried about the continual appearance of the woman, thinking that she might be a stowaway. When the guide connected the appearances with the tales of ghostly visits from Captain Mary, she no longer saw the woman in her tour group.

While it may seem startling to many individuals at first, people who have encountered Mary know and understand that she is a kind spirit that means no harm at all. The shock of coming into contact with this spirit wears off quickly when they realize how friendly she is and that she is merely overlooking the activities occurring on the *Delta Queen*. The ship has the distinction of being the only floating historic hotel in America. The ship was inducted into the National Maritime Hall of Fame in 2004.

Richard Harris Barham once noted, "Ghosts, like ladies, never speak till spoke to."

Voodoo Doctors
Along the River

So long as the stories multiply…and so few are positively explained away, it is
bad method to ignore them.
—William James, American psychologist

Guinea Sam

Water has a fascinating attraction. Flowing water gives rise to energy workings of all kinds. Booneville snuggles against the Missouri River west of Jefferson City and was home to the voodoo doctor called Guinea Sam. He is the most fabled of Missouri's masters, and it is said that he disappeared in a blue cloud of smoke after being defeated in a "conjuration" contest with a voodoo doctor from St. Louis. His real name was Sam Nightingale, and he came to Booneville in 1856, brought in by Dr. Horatio Ellis from Louisiana. He claimed to be native African, and his accent was strangely foreign. For thirty years, he conjured love potions and herbal remedies, crafted charms, played tricks on the populace and cast magic. It's said that Dr. Hunt, while making a sick call on horseback, passed near Guinea Sam's home and heard his voice rise in supplication.

Dr. Hunt dismounted, approached and peered into the cabin window. Sam was on his knees, hands raised, tears streaming in earnest down his ancient, paper-thin cheeks: "Oh Lord. I'se old and forsaken, my roots is laid, my branches is withered without no leaves hanging onto them. I'se served so many yeahs [years] I've done lost count. Take ole Sambo home oh Lord, he so tired of waiting and weary ob [of] dis wicked worl [world]. I'se ready Lord, I'se ready and long to hear that blessed trumpet of yo angel Gabriel!"

Dr. Hunt had his hunting horn with him and blew loud and long. Sam responded with a start. "Who dat?" he said, to which the good doctor answered from his hiding place, "The angel Gabriel come for Guinea Sam." Sam's immediate response was a trembling, "Guinea Sam, he–he don' live heah no more, sah, he done moved away er [a] long time ago."

Guinea Sam died on August 4, 1887, and his obituary appeared on August 5, despite the claims of his blue cloud vanishing act. Like many voodoo practitioners, he was feared as being able to cast spells and throw curses, bring bad luck, cause wayward husbands or wives to return, cause milk to sour, bring good or ill luck, cure people of ailments or drive them insane.

AUNT ETERNITY'S CURSE

This is a well-known tale that is based on a possible curse and involves an elderly slave woman. The story has been around for years. In Booneville, a great mansion was built by Thornton Muir. The Muir mansion was said be one of the most magnificent private homes in the state of Missouri. Muir's horses, carriages, uniformed servants, lavish entertainments and home were considered the grandest and most elegant trappings in Missouri.

Muir spared no expense in building his dream. Walls of hand-patted plaster and wainscoting adorned each and every room. A sweeping staircase of polished mahogany rose to connect to the upper floor. Muir held a high social position in Booneville for years. An invitation from him to dine at the Muirs' home or attend a country drive was highly coveted. When Muir's daughter, Nancy, was struck ill, even his wealth could not prevent her from succumbing to the health hazards of the day. The fast-acting malady was familiar in that era, and the illness progressed in this manner: Monday, full health; Tuesday, chills and fever; Wednesday, delirium; and Thursday or Friday, death.

Booneville's finest physician gave the girl quinine, but she did not improve; she had never before been this seriously ill. Muir called in a specialist from St. Louis who quickly prescribed medicines to "cleanse the system and lower the fever." They failed, and Muir consulted a local herb doctor, buying a brew of ginseng and wild berries. That, too, failed to heal the girl. Muir turned in sheer desperation to one of his oldest slaves, said to have magical healing powers and held in high regard by her peers.

Aunt Eternity, however, had more than one reason to harbor hostility toward the Muir family. Besides being a slave, Eternity had been accused by Nancy of stealing—possibly a guest's silk scarf, as accounted in some tales. Eternity had worked long and hard to achieve a level of position within the family's servant structure and was promptly demoted in punishment of her supposed crime. Now Eternity had lost all prestige among the other slaves and was regulated to the most menial and demeaning tasks.

Even though Eternity had suffered reproach at the hands of Nancy, she apparently tried her best to save the girl. All efforts failed. Nancy languished until she died, leaving Muir distraught, even though he and his wife appeared to accept the loss of their daughter.

However, Muir brooded over the next few weeks, convincing himself that someone had cursed his dear Nancy. He ruled out Charity (the mulatto), Tobiath (the crippled woman) and Jethro (Tobiath's husband), as well as the trusted Hazekiah. Aunt Eternity came to mind, with her baleful face, thundering voice and her sour demeanor. She lived alone in her hut on slave's row and had ruled the other slaves with an iron hand.

It is thought that he may have been under the influence of alcohol, his reasoning warped by drink and grief, when he took a horsewhip one night, strode through the fog to Aunt Eternity's cabin and beat her to death. Tales say that his steps never wavered in the shrouded swale between the main house and the cabins, and by the oil lamp, he saw Aunt Eternity sitting in a wooden chair, nodding to sleep, her open Bible in her lap. Before she could react, Muir struck her down, then she uttered curses on Muir and his family and his future generations before she died.

Muir's fortune declined, and every family member died a sudden death. The mansion decayed, the front veranda collapsing, windows falling out of the rotting frames and loose shutters hanging eerily askew. The mansion emptied. Then stories of the haunting began. It is unsure if the ghost tales started while Muir was still alive or after his demise, but the property value of his estate declined tremendously with the spread of accounts of strange lights burning in the mansion and moving from room to room. Sounds emanated from the empty house, and a misty female figure was seen standing beneath the great oak tree. She was a maiden in appearance, young, pale and languid, singing an old love song. She was also seen leaning against the dry fountain or wandering the once beautiful garden. Naturally, people claimed that the ghost was Nancy, the only member who eluded Aunt Eternity's curse.

So the tale goes, and so also is the evidence that supports the story as a fabrication, invented to see how far such a tale would spread. Is it real or an experiment in how legends begin and remain with us?

MISSOURI'S WILD CHILD: "BOOGIE MAN BILL"

Gooch's Mill, a ghost town located along the Missouri River, north of Jefferson City and in between Columbia and Bonneville, boasts the fable of a feral child. Gooch's Mill was established in about 1839 by Colonel William Dixon Gooch (1752–1856) of Louisa County, Virginia, and his wife, Matilda Chiles.

Old-timers who grew up around Gooch's Mill told a tale that circulated just below the surface of public knowledge of a person kept in a cage who howled like a wolf and growled like a bear—a person no one saw except in the shadows. Perhaps the legend is based on fact. "A fellow who lived long ago, folks around here called him 'Boogie Man Bill,' and he lived in the country by Gooch's Mill," the old-timers say.

Bob Dyer, a folk musician, poet and historian known as the "Bard of Boonville," researched the wild child legend, as well as other Missouri folk tales. Dyer was born in Boonville on May 22, 1939. He received his undergraduate and master's degrees in English from Missouri University (MU) and taught classes in English and film there. Mr. Dyer left MU after about fifteen years to pursue his passion for sharing history and tradition through folk music and books. His historical tales of mid-Missouri cover topics such as Lewis and Clark, Mark Twain's *Huckleberry Finn,* a flood of the Missouri River and the Osage and Missouri American Indians. Bob died on April 11, 2007, but studied and wrote a song about Boogie Man Bill, "The Wild Child of Gooch's Mill."

Dyer's description of him noted the following: "[S]trange and wild, and he had long hair. His clothes were ragged, and he growled like a bear. He was kept locked up in a cabin on the hill out in the country by Gooch's Mill." He spent time piecing together a tale of a boy born out of the union of the daughter of a poor black man and the son of a rich white man on a night shattered by lightning and hail.

Bill's mama died when he was born, the tale goes, and the daddy disappeared, leaving the wild child with a "Granny Woman" (a midwife). Bill was worse at the full moon, breaking free and roaming, scrounging in the hills above the mill. Some said that he drank fresh blood and howled like a wolf. Bill's end came ultimately on a Halloween night when someone "burned up 'Boogie Man Bill,'" according to the old-timers, "out in the country by Gooch's Mill." The overall impression remains that on moonlit nights, the ghost of "Boogie Man Bill" can be seen and heard atop the hill above Gooch's Mill.

The place is darker than dark, a ghost town with two graveyards (one for the white people and the other for the blacks). When there's no moon, no lights are reflected by the low-hanging clouds. There are howls of an outcast suffering physical and mental afflictions, one who had been kept shackled and who died under suspicious conditions. He wanders the hills, wailing between the tombstones.

Even today, people conduct investigations in the vicinity, trying to find the remaining evidence of the wild child or capture his cries, but so far, "Boogie Man Bill" has not cooperated in being discovered and remains elusive, true to his feral nature.

SHADOW BEINGS

B lacker than black" shades (or shadowy, humanlike figures) appear in Native American stories (such as those in Nez Perce, Cherokee and Choctaw cultures), and some of these shadow beings are said to be shape-shifters. One of these tales is about Coyote and the shadow people. Coyote's trickster character is both complex and ambiguous. A common mindset of our canine hero is one of ambivalence and inner strife, literary features usually associated with modern fiction, especially the novel. French anthropologist Claude Lévi-Strauss proposed a structured theory that suggests that Coyote and Crow obtained mythic status because they are mediator animals between life and death. "Beware the trickster" is a refrain often heard among Native Americans. Coyote seems to continually show up in the most unexpected places.

Known for its ability to adapt and live nearly anywhere, coyotes are found all over the world, in every climate and at every elevation. They live and thrive in the wilderness and alongside humans in more rural settings. They possess such a wide variety of survival skills that they stand a good chance of never becoming endangered or extinct. The "trickster" idea comes from the marvelous adaptability of the creature. Native people have observed all kinds of animals and their behavior throughout time. They've learned much about animals and the differences between them and us by watching the instinctive antics and behavior of those with which we share the natural wilderness areas. Hundreds, maybe even thousands, of coyote stories have circulated throughout Indian lands in nearly every tribe ever since anyone can remember. One tale goes as follows.

Coyote mourns for his dead wife. The death spirit takes Coyote to see her upon his promise to do just as the ghost does (the classical admonition: "You must do whatever I say; do not disobey"). Guided through a series of images and illusions that Coyote (at first confused) must acknowledge as real, he is rewarded with the arrival at the longhouse, the Lodge of Shadows, where he greets old friends. Coyote is able to see his wife and friends at night and visits with them. Finally, the ghost sends him home with his wife, whom he is forbidden to touch until he has crossed the fifth mountain, signaling the triumph over the underworld. At his last camp, he embraces her and she disappears forever. Weeping at her loss, he vainly retraces his journey, reenacting the illusions of the first trip that are now so movingly useless. Finally, he arrives back at the dusty prairie where he first encountered the Lodge of the Shadows. Thus people do not return from the dead.

Similar beings called djinn or jinn (from which we get the word "genie") date back to pre-Islamic mythology. They are also able to change their shape and are said to inhabit a parallel world to humans. Many people still believe in their existence. They are reported as staying in, or just outside of, the shadows that can normally be found in a location. Shadow people (also known as shadow beings) are usually attracted to one person or location for unknown reasons. Most often, they are seen as dark silhouettes of human shape, generally male, that prefer to watch someone unseen and flee the moment they are noticed. Shadow people are said to travel extremely rapidly and can pass through solid matter, making them less prone to direct visual contact. Their characteristics range from being diffident and playful to downright spiteful and malevolent.

Unusual descriptions from people who came across these beings in different countries all over the world have been very daunting. While some people see a shadowy humanlike form, others see formless, translucent black splotches and twirling columns of murky smoke. Described as black or gray silhouettes, they lack eyes, a mouth and facial expressions. Some individuals, though, report that they have seen shadow beings with red or yellow eyes. Shadow people lack mass and appear distorted and vaporous. They are viewed as two-dimensional and distorted and are known to be very quick and disjointed in their movements. Others have described their movement as being like a "dance" from one wall to the next. Their movements are sometimes described as "unnatural." Sometimes they are said to move in slow motion, as if they were submerged in liquid, and then suddenly move rapidly from one place to another within the room. They have often been reported as being childlike, playing games with witnesses. These seem to be curious and are also almost always seen through peripheral vision. When the witness turns to see them, rather than disappear through a wall or into thin air, they usually flee in a particular direction.

On the other hand, ghosts are said to be the disembodied spirits of deceased people and usually reported to take on the appearance and characteristics of human beings. Orbs of light, ectoplasm or glowing mists can be associated with ghost sightings.

The most common type is the human type shadow person. These entities are described as generally humanoid in shape and size, with anatomical details reading like a grocery list: no eyes and all shadow, empty eyes (holes where the eyes should be, allowing you to look straight through), red eyes, green eyes, blue lights for eyes, eyes that change to all sorts of colors and no hands or feet. Size can range from two feet to six feet; shape can be humanoid, "blobs," shadow animals or spherical balls; gender can be apparent (squared shoulders associated to men, and shadow breasts from the side have been reported, though the reports lean more toward male encounters) or not; feelings waft from the beings (from calm watchfulness to immobilizing fear and dread); and definition of form (from seeing five distinct fingers to seeing a blur for hands) can all be different from case to case.

Interestingly, some reports claim that shadow beings can wear a distinct hat, hold a cigar or cigarette, carry a purse or bag, have horns, hold a walking cane and/or carry a pitcher or basin or some other distinguishing object. These might fall under the category of the "Hat Man" type. The Hat Man shadow person is a variation of the humanlike being described earlier. While the experiences and description of this type of entity closely matches those of the plain shadow person, there are noticeable differences, the most obvious being the inclusion of a wide-brimmed hat in witness descriptions. The hat worn by this type of shadow person is described variably as having a brim the width of the creature's shoulders. In other instances, the description of this creature mimics that of the human-shaped variety. The Hat Man seems to exhibit a certain degree of curiosity toward the witnesses involved in sighting it or him, whichever the case may be. There have been occasional reports of dread and paralysis associated with this creature, but to a much lesser degree than those associated with the black smoke shadow being.

I had my own experience with the "Hat Man" type of shadow being. My daughter Charlene and three other friends had been called to a location outside of Columbia, Missouri, to do a cleansing on the land. This was once Native American territory, with cliff paintings not far from our location. Rumors claimed that bad magic, or possibly some form of misconstrued voodoo, had been cast on the land, and the entire area seemed afflicted with dread. Black figures were reported to have been falling from the trees, and snaky, demonlike forms had been seen in the barn on the property. A female ghost occupied one of the houses, appearing both as a younger woman and as aged as when she died. During the day, we walked the property line and felt the blockages placed on the land. At night, we were called outside to the back deck. Interstate 70 traffic was visible beyond the small valley, with the lights of the truck and cars appearing clearly. The outside light was on and illuminated the deck; however, the immediate yard beyond was in complete and total blackness past the deck's wooden railing. It was as if we were staring into a void. Photos taken of that backyard showed a small, seemingly male figure wearing what resembled, for all intents and purposes, a leprechaun-style hat. This area may have been home to the little people of Indian lore. Subsequent photos taken from right to left of the area showed the being moving in progress across the end of the yard up next to the tree line that marked the beginning of a cliff dropping off into the valley below. While I was standing on the deck, the backyard suddenly became fully illuminated as the outdoor lighting reached across the yard and into the tree line behind the house.

Later that night, after my daughter had already gone to sleep (we shared a bed, one of our companions slept on the couch and the couple with us was in the other guestroom), I decided to call it a day. No sooner had I lain down than someone began tugging the blankets off me. My daughter did not stir on her side of the bed. I pulled them up, and again the blankets were tugged away from me. I was wide awake when this occurred. All night I struggled with the feeling of someone standing right next to me, hovering at my knees. The next morning, I told the others about my sleepless night, beginning with the blankets being pulled off me. They each had their own tales of sighting the Hat Man or vivid dreams of him hovering over them. This hatted man haunted all five of us throughout the night, either in dreams or in the sight of him standing at our bedsides.

Who was he? Did he serve the purpose of a guardian that night in face of the earlier strangeness outside? Or was he merely taking our measure quietly, hoping to frighten us? We still have no answer for the evening's events, but maybe the Hat Man will pay another visit in the future.

The duration of the sighting of this type of shadow person varies among reports but is usually stated as between two and five seconds. At times, my own experiences have lasted longer. Many witnesses describe the sensation of being watched, with the shadow forms often first seen on the side of one's vision (peripheral vision). Many cannot pinpoint when the feeling of being watched starts, but the feeling grows before the being is spotted, often in a corner of the room, a darkened doorway or behind them. Once the person notices the odd out-of-place feeling and focuses attention on the shadow, it is either seen to move out of sight or disappear/blend in with the other shadows; sometimes it is described as being denser than the surrounding shadows. The phrase "It seemed to absorb the light" has been used more than once. Looking up to see if someone is in the room, the witness discovers the shadow person observing him or her. Once noticed, the shadow person seems to flee quite rapidly, sometimes traveling through walls or closed doors. I have had the fortune of staring straight at some of the shadow beings, as well as having sightings in my peripheral vision.

The standard saying, "dispersed and reformed" describes movements. If the being leaves and doesn't come back, most cases state that the shadow "dispersed and seemingly blended with the shadows surrounding it" or "darted away and disappeared." The vast majority of repeat-encounter cases note that people "feel" the being's thoughts focused on them. The phrase "It's hard to explain" is used a lot in relation to this aspect.

The more consistent accounts of shadow people typically describe a feeling of dread associated with the presence of this phenomenon, and animals are said to react to the phenomena with fear and hostility. Being touched by a shadow being can leave a person feeling drained and fatigued, and these feelings can vary. Some have described the sensation of being touched to equal that of getting touched by a high-voltage electric fence, while some feel a warm invasion—as if it doesn't so much as touch the skin as it goes through and into it. A majority of cases involve the shadow being coming from or going into a closet, sometimes repeatedly. In my account earlier, the couple in the guestroom said that the Hat Man went into the closet and disappeared.

Many cases also mention them going (or diving) under beds or seemingly flying up through a ceiling. The shadows will be seen for weeks or months in a row and then be gone again.

The second most common type of shadow person reported is that of the black smoke or black mist type. At first, it may seem odd to label these entities as "people," but in many cases, witnesses who have encountered these beings have described them as having intelligent characteristics and reactions to events. Strangely, many of the encounters with the black smoke shadow beings have been associated with overwhelming feelings of dread and malevolence, much more so than the experiences related to the human-shaped variety.

The majority of reports state that one or two adults at most witness the shadow being encounter. Mass sightings with more witnesses are rare. Sightings by children often occur, especially in the case of brothers/ sisters who may share the same encounter(s).

Some shadow beings seem aggressive. Some cause utter terror in people, to the point that they feel paralyzed with fear. Many who encounter this type of shadow being later state that it was the shadow projecting the fear and aggression and not the person involved. Some claim that horrible thoughts fly through their minds as they looked at the shadow. These shadows also seem to be less fearful of being seen and have, in fact, been reported as being brazen in their entrance into an area and their direct approach to the person involved, walking through furniture or walls to get to a person. Aggressive shadow being reports come from adults as well as children, so there does not seem to be a distinction, though many would probably theorize that children would be more afraid by any shadow being—that does not seem to be the case. Reports of being touched by or of having a shadow being reaching out are not as common as reports of sightings. Perhaps that is why only a few shadow beings are labeled aggressive. Some seemingly common factors of aggressive shadow being encounters include the following:

✠   One person is involved.

✠   If another person walking in on the shadow interrupts the "attack," the shadow disperses quickly, sometimes taking the time to look at the intruder before going.

✠   Horrible feelings are reported by "victims" of shadow being "attacks," such as icy darkness closing in on them, panic over not being able to move, terror, unbelievable sadness, heightened sense of awareness (to the point of pain) and/ or feeling like you are touching an electric fence (vibrating painfully).

✠   Sharp pain, not always localized; it has been reported as "zooming around the body."

Lingering after the attack is a residual fear that another one might happen in the future, to the point of paranoia and the feeling of not wanting to be left alone. According to the reports of these "attacks," the encounters are not taken lightly, and they can leave lasting effects. In few cases, some report bruising or cuts left by the entity. This does not happen enough to be investigated properly, however, and on the few occasions of a shadow being attack, reports suggest that something had apparently triggered it. This is most often stated when the person had seen the shadow being before the attack though no contact was attempted—sometimes for years before an attack occurs. Are these attacks psychological, or do some shadow beings suddenly become aggressive?

Other beings—called the "Watchers"—seem to just observe events and never attempt physical contact. These shadow people can stay around for years, even generations without ever attempting contact with a person. Watchers are most often reported as being seen out of the corner of one's eyes, to the side of a room—observing from a distance, following a person (and disappearing as soon as they are noticed) or standing in the existing shadows of a room or doorway. For the vast majority of watcher reports, there is no feeling of aggression coming from them. At most, a sense or presence is felt, and when the shadow is spotted, they often vanish immediately or fade quickly into their surroundings. Several reports of watchers include an entity coming upon them when they appear to be looking at or studying an open book or upon a sleeping individual or a person looking at papers on a table/desk or at art/pictures on a wall. When watchers are found in such positions, the majority either seem surprised that they were "caught" and disperse or swing to look at the person who "caught" them and then whisk away. Many of these cases leave the person who witnessed the encounter stunned but not afraid, more curious than anything. Some seemingly common factors among watchers include the following:

✛ They appear content to simply watch what is going on around them.

✠ They may not always be present and can, in fact, be sporadic in their appearances, with sometimes days, weeks, months or years between "visits."

✠ More than one person often senses and then spots a watcher at the same time.

✠ Locations that seem to have a resident watcher generally do not report feelings of fear, although the word "creepy" is often used.

✠ Watchers do not seem to be limited to showing up only for quiet family moments and are often photographed to the side of or in the backgrounds of parties and family get-togethers.

✠ Rarely do watchers allow themselves to be fully seen and noticed.

✠ If approached, watchers seem to want to avoid contact, as they more often than not either disappear or turn and leave.

Watchers on the whole do not seem to be viewed as a threat, and many who have resident watchers will tell you that although they get a little creeped out at times, they generally do not mind the presence.

The "little guys" are only two to four feet tall. This type, interestingly enough, is most often reported in locations that are already thought to be haunted by another spirit/entity. Many of these "children" are reported in haunted location across Missouri, as well as in other states. Nobody has really theorized a reason for this as yet. But that could be because the tiny things are quick little buggers. Very few reports can clearly describe them as they move so fast. If anything, this type of shadow being is disconcerting and extremely hard to investigate. The popular TV show *Ghost Hunters* (on the Syfy channel) seems to have a fair amount of run-ins with this type of shadow being and has recorded some interesting footage of what they believe is a short shadow being. Some seemingly common factors among little guys include the following:

✝ They are very fast, almost like a blur.

✝ They are often seen zipping by the person who encounters them or off in the distance, perhaps flying by a doorway or "running" across the end of a room.

✝ They are more often found in locations thought to be haunted by something else.

✝ An unusual number of sightings occur in bedrooms, often around the foot of a bed.

✝ They are usually described as a waist-high shadow that is slightly pudgy. More detail than that is rare due to their speed.

✝ Sightings of these little guys seem to be less frequent than that of watchers.

The difficulty of obtaining good visuals of these tiny ones remains a large mystery in the paranormal field. Researchers are perplexed as to how to set up investigations to try and capture little guys, as many do not seem to have scheduled appearances at locations or even regular places where they are seen throughout the location. Of the few pictures and video recordings that have been reported, only a small percentage actually tries to catch the shadow being.

What types don't fit into the other categories? These include, but are not limited to, shadow spheres, geometric shapes, shadow animals, blobs, shadow "sticks" (visible heads but no arms or legs, just a line of shadow), shadow doors (when spotted, they can be watched for several minutes before closing), rogue shadows (shadows seen going from one place to another in the middle of nowhere) and flat shadows (no depth and normally only seen once). As opposed to humanoid-shaped shadow beings, these are much rarer and harder to investigate.

Since all of these occurrences vary, it would be hard to put together a list of things to look for in most of the cases. Some examples of what happened when these various types were encountered include seeing a shadow ball roll down a hall or stairs, seeing a nearly six-foot-tall tall shadow with a triangular head and long downward-pointing triangular body, spotting a shadow door (rectangle) underneath a tree in broad daylight and watching it close after several minutes, watching a shadow dog leap into and across one room and disappear into the next, seeing a shadow "blob" move across a wall and break up into smaller blobs that scattered around the room and seeing a flat shadow make quite a show of turning sideways to avoid being seen by three witnesses.

One type of shadow creature is much less common than the human-shaped or smoke varieties. Sightings of these creatures have described vaguely animal-like forms of a dark and semitransparent appearance. Many witnesses have described them as being roughly the size of a rabbit or guinea pig. These creatures have been witnessed indoors and outdoors equally and exhibit some of the otherworldly qualities of other types of shadow beings, such as the ability to travel through solid matter and unnatural speed. Nearly every shadow animal has the distinction of being described as "catlike" or of possessing such characteristics. Some report that shadow animals appear to be a hybrid between a cat and some other creature. They always move incredibly quickly. The viewer usually realizes what has happened after they are spotted and have left the area.

Stories have a sense of flight to them. The shadow animal is seen and then suddenly flees, realizing that it has been noticed. Other cases describe shadow animals as scampering through a location. Unlike shadow people, shadow animals do not leave harboring feelings of negativity. They may leave a sense of surprise and possibly urgency in their flight, but they do not appear malicious. The intent of shadow animals is unknown. Some believe that they are animal souls passing through to the next phase (i.e., reincarnation), but there is simply no known pattern as to who spots them, when or why or what seeing a shadow animal means. Rarely is the face of the animal seen or reported. Usually, general features of the body are noticed, but the face is missing, faded or obscured.

My own encounters with shadows beings are varied. I've chased full-bodied shadow people only to have them "blend" in with the surroundings. I've seen a solid shadow "man" standing in front of my house, beneath a streetlamp, staring at us through the front screen door after my middle daughter and a high school friend made an ill-advised venture to a haunted location nearby known as "Satan's Tunnel." The two girls came home shaken and frightened by whatever they experienced there, and as they recalled their account of the trip, I experienced that "creeped out" feeling, glanced out the door and saw the shadow man lurking at the edge of my home's property boundary. This to date has been my only encounter with a shadow being that in any way felt "malevolent." I called the girls' attention to the being and mentally told it that it could not breach the boundaries of my property. The thing stood stock still, staring (as it were, since no eyes were visible). Then, while we looked straight at it, the shadow being was suddenly gone. It didn't move or fade; it was simply no longer there, gone from beneath the bright streetlight without a movement.

Shadow children have shown up in photographs I've taken on locations said to be haunted and where children have historically been recorded to have died. Flat shadows have flowed over walls in places such as the "Villisca Axe Murder House" in Iowa during an investigation in which I participated. Even shadow animals have been around me. I've seen cats, large birds and other amorphous shapes. Other people have witnessed a shadow cat following me when no living cat existed in the vicinity.

There have been occasions when doing an investigation in a home where no children or animals have been present that not only have I witnessed shadow children and cats, but there are also audible recordings of a child's voice and a cat's meowing. During my first visit to one location, a photograph captured the image of a white mist touching my cheek at the precise place and time when I felt a cold, small, childlike finger touch my face. I've been told that an EVP was also captured of my name being called. A "Where's Janice?" in what appeared to be a young girl's voice was recorded when I failed to make a return visit at a time schedule for another investigation. At this site, there was no power, running water, bathroom facilities, children, animals or any living soul, as the building was under renovation. Upon a return visit to the same location, what seemed to be a young girl was noted as both a shadow figure and a white, mist-like apparition.

I've watch shadow creatures walk upright as in human form, fly or strut about on all fours, some gliding across the top of the walls, just below the ceiling, and others scurrying at the floorboards in rat-like shapes or in some other small mammalian forms. Many of these sightings are found in the state of Missouri.

JEFFERSON CITY

The territory of Missouri was acquired as part of the 1803 Louisiana Purchase and became a state in 1821 as part of the Missouri Compromise. Jefferson City was named in honor of President Thomas Jefferson, who envisioned an expanding America. In pre-Columbian times, this region was home to an ancient group of people known only as the Mound Builders. By the time European settlers began arriving here, the Mound Builders had already vanished into history and the indigenous peoples then present were called the Osage Indians.

Known as simply Jeff or Jeff City to residents, the city is located just to the left of center in the state, almost midway between Missouri's two largest cities, Kansas City and St. Louis. It is located north of Springfield, another Missouri metropolitan area, and is easily accessible from most parts of the state. When the Missouri Territory was organized in 1812, St. Louis was the seat of government. St. Charles served as the capital until Jefferson City was chosen as the new capital in 1821. It is the county seat of Cole County. Part of the city is in Callaway County, Missouri.

In 1821, Jefferson City was known as Lohman's Landing. When the city was first chosen to be the state capital, they proposed the name

View from the Missouri River at Jefferson City, vintage postcard. *Courtesy Janice Tremeear.*

"Missouriopolis" but later settled on Jefferson City. It was little more than a trading post located in the wilderness about midway between St. Louis and Kansas City. In 1826, the Missouri legislature first met here. In 1839, the site was incorporated as a city. The state capital sits on the Missouri River near the geographic center of the state and is dominated by a beautiful domed capitol, rising from a bluff overlooking the Missouri River. Lewis and Clark passed beneath that bluff on their historic expedition.

The Missouri River is an important part of Jeff City history. The oldest portions of the town can be found at the Jefferson Landing State Historic Site on Jefferson Street along the river and below the state capitol. Like most river towns, Jefferson City was founded on the active river trade of the late eighteenth and nineteenth centuries. Historic displays about the city's early history can be found at the site. Three buildings compose the site: the 1839 Lohman Building, which includes a museum and visitor center; the 1854 Christopher Maus House; and the 1855 Union Hotel. The heart of the city's history can be found here and at the state capitol just up the hill. Jefferson City is also located along the two-hundred-mile-long Katy Trail that travels from St. Charles, Missouri, to outside Sedalia, Missouri. The Katy Trail runs along the path once taken by the Missouri, Kansas and Texas Railroad and runs beside the Missouri River.

By 1826, the capital was a growing commercial and transportation hub, serving as a transfer point for goods and passengers. Incorporated as a city in 1839, it was a significant year in the history of the capital for another reason.

That same year, a three-story stone structure was built on the riverfront by James A. Crump that would serve as a tavern, hotel, telegraph office, grocery store, warehouse and brothel during its history. Crump sold the central and eastern sections to three men and kept the western basement section to use as the grocery store. The double doors on the ground level faced the river, making it convenient for freight to be loaded on and off steamboats.

He sold the eastern section to John Yount and the central section to E.B. Cordell and James Dunnica. He then leased the upper floors from the three co-owners and opened the Missouri House hotel. This hotel was known as the largest and most comfortable lodging for members of the

First capital riverfront landing, vintage postcard. *Courtesy Janice Tremeear.*

legislature and for social events in the area; it became known generally as "the landing." Crump's hotel earned a reputation as a meeting place for river men.

In 1852, Charles Maus and his brother-in-law, Charles Lohman, bought the eastern section of Crump's building and used it for a general store. The upper floors could no longer accommodate the hotel traffic, so in 1855, Charles Maus built another hotel across from the Missouri House hotel. He changed the name of his new hotel to the Veranda Hotel and then, upon his return home from the Civil War, renamed it the Union Hotel to match his political sentiments.

Maus and Lohman ended their business partnership in 1859 with Lohman buying the two remaining sections of Crump's building (thus the name change to the Lohman Building). Charles Lohman then developed one of the area's largest warehouse and trade businesses at the site.

With the coming of the Pacific Railroad, business boomed in the 1850s. The capital city became the transfer point for goods coming from the east by rail and heading west by steamboat. Much of this activity occurred at the landing. In 1852, Charles Maus and his brother-in-law, Charles Lohman, bought the eastern section of Crump's building and opened a general store. In response to a growing demand for hotel accommodations, Maus built a hotel across the street from Crump's building in 1855. His brother, Christopher Maus, built a home a few yards south of the hotel. The sturdy brick house exemplifies the small, red brick residences common in Jefferson City during this time period.

After the war, river traffic slowed as the railroad offered cheaper and faster transportation. In the 1870s, both Lohman and Maus relocated their businesses away from the landing.

The Pacific Railroad reached Jefferson City late in 1855. West from that point, the railroad was purposefully located away from the Missouri River to avoid competition with steamboat traffic. The Pacific Railroad itself established a fleet of twelve steamboats to connect with the trains at Jefferson City and transport passengers and freight on up the river to Kansas City and beyond. An advertisement of that period stated that at Jefferson City passengers could step from the train to the waiting steamboat and that, by this route, the time from St. Louis to Kansas City had been cut to a mere fifty hours. In the 1870s, both Lohman and Maus relocated their businesses away from the landing. The Union Hotel and the Lohman Building were used as storage and tenements until the early twentieth century, when they became a factory and offices for the Tweedie Shoe Company.

The state acquired the property in the 1960s, with the initial intent of building a parking lot, but concerned citizens led by Elizabeth Rozier spearheaded a movement to preserve the buildings. The Lohman Building was placed on the National Register of Historic Places in 1969, and in 1974, the state's bicentennial commission adopted the Jefferson Landing proposal as the state's official bicentennial project. Three structures on the property—the Lohman Building, the Union Hotel and the Christopher Maus House next door to them—were restored. The Lohman Building was opened to the public on July 4, 1976, as the cornerstone of the Jefferson Landing Historic Site.

State capitol, postcard. *Courtesy Janice Tremeear.*

The Jefferson Landing State Historic Site is significant as a rare Missouri River landing. The Lohman Building features exhibits on transportation and a film on the history of the capital city. It also serves as a support facility for the Missouri State Museum, located on the main floor of the capitol. The Union Hotel houses the Elizabeth Rozier Gallery, with rotating exhibits emphasizing Missouri's history, art and culture. The ground floor of the former hotel keeps up the tradition of providing transportation to the heartland of the state by serving as the city's Amtrak train station. The area at the base of Jefferson Street, known as Jefferson's Landing, was the site of the original river landing and the first area settled in the city. It is significant as a rare surviving Missouri River landing place. The structures in this historic site date back to 1839, making it the oldest riverfront landing on the Missouri River. As this site was later served by the railroad, several of Jefferson City's largest businesses grew here.

STATE CAPITOL

Many years ago on a tour of the state capitol at Jeff City, we were told of a ghostly vision roaming the halls. Who or what this spirit represents seems unclear, but the domed building has a rich history of its own. The first state capitol building in Jefferson City was built in the period of 1823–26 and was destroyed by fire in 1837. A new capitol building had been approved at the time and was completed in 1840. The second capitol was destroyed by fire on February 5, 1911, when a bolt of lightning struck the dome. The present capitol was built in the period of 1913–17 and stands on the same spot as its predecessor, high atop a bluff overlooking the Missouri River. The structure, covering nearly three acres, is a symmetrical building of the Roman Renaissance style, surmounted by a dome of unusual beauty. It stands upon 285 concrete piers, which extend to solid rock at depths from 20 to 50 feet. It is 437 feet long and 200 feet wide through the

Interior view of the state capitol, vintage postcard. *Courtesy Janice Tremeear.*

wings. The exterior is of Carthage, Missouri limestone marble, as are the floors of all the corridors, the rotundas and the treads of the stairways. There are 134 columns in the building, totaling one-fourth of the stone used in the entire structure.

The grand stairway is one of the capitol's outstanding features. It is thirty feet wide and extends from the front portico to the third floor. It is more than sixty-five feet from the wall on one side of the stairway to the wall on the other side. At the entrance is a mammoth bronze front door, thirteen feet by eighteen feet.

Atop the lantern of the capitol dome, 260 feet above the ground, is a classic bronze figure of Ceres, goddess of grain, chosen to symbolize the state's great agricultural heritage.

As Missouri's seat of government during the Civil War, Jefferson City witnessed many exciting and dramatic scenes. During the early months of the war, the opposing forces of secession and unionism engaged in a tense contest for dominance that culminated in the hasty evacuation of the elected pro-Southern government and its replacement by a military-backed provisional Federal government. Once the North

Left: General Ulysses S. Grant, vintage postcard. *Courtesy Janice Tremeear.*

Below: Reenactment of Civil War soldiers doing the porcupine maneuver, Springfield, Missouri. *Photo by Dean Pestana.*

gained the upper hand, defense of the strategically important city became a vital priority as the provisional government struggled to maintain a semblance of control in a deeply divided and war-torn state. As the Civil War moved into its later stages, the capital was menaced with the threat of attack by Confederate horsemen—by Colonel Joseph Shelby's raiders in late 1863 and by General Sterling Price's army one year later. Decisions made in Jefferson City affected the course of the war in every part of the state. Most major Civil War figures in Missouri, including Generals Grant, Fremont, Price and Lyons, lived in Jefferson City sometime during the war.

Missouri entered in the Union in 1821 as a slave state, and pro-Southerners controlled state government for four decades. As the nation drew close to war in early 1861, Missouri governor Claiborne Fox Jackson openly sided with secession from the Union. After the Civil War began on April 12, 1861, Jackson tried to convince the Missouri General Assembly to secede. But pro-Union troops took over the state militia and Federal arsenal in St. Louis in May and then came immediately to Jefferson City, seizing the capital city and keeping state government in pro-Union hands. Governor Jackson and pro-Confederacy officials fled south before the pro-Union troops

General Sterling Price, vintage postcard.
Courtesy Janice Tremeear.

arrived, and his "rump" legislature of Southern sympathizers later voted in absentia for secession.

Those majority legislators who remained in Jefferson City in July 1861 elected their own governor, Hamilton Gamble, and voted to keep Missouri in the Union. After these first few months of confusion, Jefferson City remained securely in Union hands, under the protection of hundreds of state and Federal troops garrisoned there. Jefferson City had only 3,082 residents in 1860, including some 300 slaves. During the war years, as many as 15,000 federal troops were stationed at one time in Jefferson City, creating an enormous logistical problem of providing food and water for the troops and their horses. Troop camps of thousands of men ringed the town. Others were quartered on the grounds of the capitol and penitentiary.

In addition, Jefferson City swarmed at times with refugees fleeing bushwhackers in the surrounding counties and seeking safe havens. Townspeople and local farmers did their best to supply both troops and refugees. Jefferson City also took in hundreds of wounded soldiers during the war. Churches and private homes were pressed into service as "hospitals." Those who died provided the impromptu beginnings in 1861 of what would become a national cemetery after the war. The dark capitol basement served as a "dungeon" for prisoners.

While you may find an employee or tour guide who will mention the "ghost," you probably won't get a confirmation that the capitol is haunted.

OTHER LOCATIONS AROUND JEFFERSON CITY

Other areas in or around Jefferson City have their own ghost stories, too, such as the following places.

Wainwright Bridge

Strange reports of Wainwright Bridge note people parking their cars on the bridge at midnight, turning the engines off and (allegedly) having their cars slowly roll off the bridge. Odd noises can be heard below the bridge, as if someone is beating on it or scratching the steal support beams. There have been bloody footprints spotted leading out of the water into the mud, only to stop abruptly, as if the person leaving the footprints simply disappeared. A dozen missing persons have been reported as having been last seen near or on the bridge, and three bodies of farmers have been found below it. A car drove off one side of the bridge and landed a dozen or so yards on the other side.

Old 94

This stretch of old highway on the outskirts of Jefferson City, Missouri, is notorious for being haunted. The road is lined by cornfields, and there is a light that follows you for about four or five miles. The ghost of a mischievous old man named Ofie is known to haunt the road. Several people have reported hitting a person on that road, getting out of their vehicles and searching for someone, only to find nothing. If you turn around on the road, you may be followed by a mysterious creature.

Old 94 Bridge

The second bridge on the Old 94 highway is hard to find, but it does exist. Local rumor has it that during the Civil War, members of an entire family of white abolitionists were hanged on the bridge, including the young twin son and daughter, who were no more than seven or eight years old. Sounds of screaming and children laughing can be heard, and wet footprints have been reported appearing in front of cars on the bridge.

Bikers who mount their ten-speeds report that they traverse many bridges erected during the Civil War times that seem to be haunted. The stories sent to me have eerie coincidences: "Seems many people crash on this one particular bridge, Old 94 Bridge…never heard of any crashes during a ride on this route that did *not* occur on this bridge." They term them "ghost territories" along their ride, and it appears that strange experiences and sightings have occurred in other locations, too. Perhaps the Old 94 Bridge is hazardous to your health.

St. Mary's Road

The eerie sound of a horse and buggy driving by, with the noise repeating three to five times, is reported in this area. You can hear the horse hooves with metal shoes hitting what sounds like stone—the wheels going around, bumping and squeaking, coming toward you, going past you and then continuing down the road.

Unknown mist anomalies captured in a photo at a haunted location. Images taken before and after this photo show no mist, and a "cold air breath test" was done for comparison. Such images often manifest in photos where ghosts are said to be present. *Photo by Charlene Wells.*

Author during a graveyard investigation. Many sightings take place in graveyards throughout Missouri. Civil War soldiers, convicted killers, mourners, children, strange animals and unexplained mists are included in the reports of activity. *Photo by Dean Pestana.*

Riverview Cemetery

Located at 2600 West Main Street in Jefferson City, Missouri, this is not the most lavish cemetery, but visitors have found photos with figures standing next to them near the tombstone, including one who said, "The picture clearly showed a woman standing off to the right of the mausoleum. It also showed streaks of light shooting into frame from the right."

GOVERNOR'S MANSION

M issouri's state capital is haunted, if you believe the legend handed down from 1993.

Designed by architect George Ingham Barnett, the mansion was constructed in 1871 for $75,000. It sits on manicured grounds and presents great character and history to those who view it. During its initial construction, the mansion was once referred to as a "jewel in a pigsty" because of the primitive living conditions surrounding the area in which it was built.

The Governor's Mansion is perched on a bluff within walking distance of the state capitol. An outstanding example of Renaissance Revival–style architecture, the mansion has been beautifully restored. The three-story red brick building is trimmed in stone and boasts an imposing portico complete with four stately pink granite columns; its mansard roof is crowned by iron grillwork. The art of Missouri painters Thomas Hart Benton and George Caleb Bingham adorns the walls, and the mansion is decked out as a haunted house at Halloween, as well as ornately decorated at holiday season.

Today, the Governor's Mansion attracts sixty thousand visitors each year who enjoy guided tours of the rooms, with the exception of the attic. The attic's exemption from the tour is no surprise. There's no reason to visit here, as it's used just for storage. But the attic does indeed have a history, and it's not one that involves matters of state or political intrigue, quiet hanky-panky or even strange scientific experiments. The attic's history is paranormal. It is theorized that the hauntings there draw from the past lives of the Crittenden family.

A repairman working on ductwork in the attic saw an eight-year-old or nine-year-old "golden-haired" girl playing nearby. She wore a white dress and lingered in the attic most of the day. When he reported the child, he was told that no little girl was present. A search proved that no children had been on the grounds at that time. This was during Christopher Bond's term as governor, and the Bonds didn't have a daughter.

The child is assumed to be Carrie, the daughter of Governor Thomas Crittenden.

Thomas Theodore Crittenden was the governor of Missouri from 1881 to 1885. He was a Civil War veteran, an attorney and the man who put up a $10,000 award for the capture of Jesse James, an offer that soon led to the robber's death. Frank James surrendered to Governor Crittenden. By

Governor's Mansion, Jefferson City, Missouri, postcard. *Courtesy Janice Tremeear.*

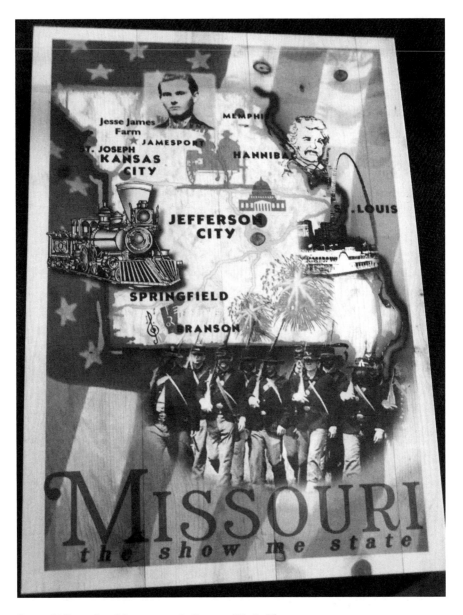

State of Missouri and flag, postcard. *Courtesy of Janice Tremeear.*

any definition, Crittenden was a strong personality and not accustomed to being weakened by severity of circumstance. Kidnappers threatened to take Carrie while Crittenden struggled to put a halt to bandit activity, and he posted bodyguards.

However, Crittenden was also the father of a little girl named Carrie, who was the love of his life, but for all his power and care, he couldn't stop disease from taking his daughter, and he was devastated when his precious daughter died of diphtheria in 1882 (some reports give 1883 as the date), as did many children of that time.

Carrie has not been reported inside the mansion since that first sighting. There are other occurrences, however. Objects move, and candles melt down to puddles of wax moments after being lit. Laughter is heard, and the elevator travels on its own. Other people died in the mansion, although Carrie was the first.

Mrs. Alexander Dockery was nearly an invalid when she arrived at the mansion, but she continued to be active. Mary Elizabeth Bird was the daughter of Greenup Bird and Catherine Pixlee. She married Dr. Alexander Dockery, who became governor of the state of Missouri. The former Mary Bird died at the executive mansion on January 1, 1903.

Governor John Sappington Marmaduke served in the Confederate army, and while camping across the river, he told his fellow officers that he would one day live in the mansion. All three died during the holiday season and lay in state with the festive decorations. Who knows what causes the unexplained oddities that happen within the Governor's Mansion.

MISSOURI STATE PENITENTIARY

Opened in 1836, the Missouri State Penitentiary underwent expansion until 1888. It was named the largest prison in the world and bore the nickname "The Wall." It reaffirmed Jefferson City as the capital of Missouri and was the oldest continuously operating prison west of the Mississippi River when it was closed in 2004, to be replaced by the modern Missouri State Correctional Facility. After almost 170 years of operation, the possibilities of paranormal activity are amazingly promising. Several visitors since the prison opened for tours have seen a woman wearing gray in the women's prison area on more than one occasion. Riots occurred in the 1950s, and a series of assaults occurred in the early 1960s, earning it the reputation of being one of the most violent prisons in the country.

With its notorious history and number of deaths on site, the prison is ripe for ghostly visits. Murders took place inside the walls. One inmate was chased through the courtyard by another wielding a shank. The unfortunate man was backed against the wall in the flower bed and stabbed to death.

A dungeon is located beneath the housing unit. Half of it was converted into showers, but the untouched portion still holds shackles. Inmates were kept for months in the large, cave-like cells in total

Old Missouri State Penitentiary, vintage postcard. *Courtesy Janice Tremeear.*

darkness, often resulting in permanent blindness. A gas chamber is part of the new tour, located in a small building outside the courtyard. Thirty-nine people were executed in the gas chamber, and now visitors can see the site that claimed so many lives.

In its 170-year history, the penitentiary played host to various notorious criminals. In the 1880s, a man caught the public's attention with his antics in prison. That man was "Firebug" (or "Desperado") Johnson, called by prison officials one of the most notorious of all the inmates ever to serve a sentence at the penitentiary. Johnson was first seen at the prison in 1882, serving a twelve-year sentence for a robbery committed in Shelby County. Earlier, he had been accused of murdering two people in Jackson County but had beaten those charges. Johnson's record of mischief began at the Shelby County Jail, as the sheriff revealed, "Johnson was a bad man and would cause trouble. While in jail here he struck the jailer over the head with a missile and came within an inch of killing him. A short time after this, he broke jail and in so doing, fell and broke his leg."

On December 25, 1895, "Stagger Lee" Shelton shot and killed William Lyons in St. Louis in the Bill Curtis Saloon. The crime Lee Shelton committed became the basis for the murder ballad "Stagger Lee." (See *Wicked St. Louis* for my account of Stagger Lee's story.)

After two trials, Shelton was convicted and sent to the state penitentiary on October 7, 1897. He helped the prison officials capture a "systematic thief" and had the support of a few powerful Democrats in the state, helping him to gain parole close to Thanksgiving 1909. Shelton was later convicted of robbery and assault and returned to prison on May 7, 1911. He was ill with tuberculosis, and after a failed attempt at a pardon, he died in prison on March 11, 1912, and was buried in an unmarked grave in St. Louis.

Charles "Pretty Boy" Floyd robbed a Kroger store/warehouse in St. Louis on September 11, 1925. He was given a three-and-a-half-year sentence. Once he left the state penitentiary, he headed to Kansas City and robbed banks. On June 7, 1933, it is rumored that Floyd linked up with Vernon Miller and Adam Richetti; they attempted to free Frank Nash from federal custody. Four officers and Nash wound up dead in what became known as the Kansas City Massacre. Floyd denied any participation in the event. In October 1934, he was tracked to a farm in Clarkson, Ohio, and killed in a shootout with law enforcement officers.

One convict in particular captured the attention of prison officials in 1899. He was from Kansas City and had just arrived at the penitentiary to serve his fifth term. Known by the nickname "Shoo-Fly," he freely admitted to being a thief and said that he would, given the chance, "steal anything that is loose at both ends and not securely nailed down." Local reporters and prison officials alike found his honesty charming, as most other convicts denied their crimes and vehemently declared their innocence throughout their prison term.

Shoo-Fly was well known as a convict who was polite, not a troublemaker, and someone who would procure for people any article requested. All that Shoo-Fly needed was a little time, and he would soon appear with the item, no matter how bizarre or unusual the request. He was proud of his ability, and prison employees had great fun testing his prowess.

Sonny Liston was convicted in 1950 of armed robbery in St. Louis and sentenced to five years in the penitentiary. Sonny Liston learned to box while in the prison, with public boxing matches held periodically. He was paroled after two years, and on September 25, 1962, he knocked out Floyd Patterson in the first round, making him the heavyweight champion of the world. He held the title for two years, until February 25, 1964, when he quit against Cassius Clay (Muhammad Ali).

James Earl Ray Jr., the man who assassinated Martin Luther King Jr., was held in the housing unit. Ray was incarcerated in the Missouri State Penitentiary after robbing a Kroger store in 1959. He was a habitual offender and was sentenced to twenty years. In 1967, he worked in the prison's bakery and squeezed into a four-by-four box. Another convict layered bread on top of the box, and it was loaded onto a truck leaving the prison. Guards failed to conduct a thorough search, and Ray escaped on April 23, 1967. One year later, on April 4, 1968, Ray assassinated Dr. Martin Luther King Jr. in Memphis, Tennessee.

While youthful and energetic entrepreneurs named Priesmeyer, Bruns, Houchin, Parker, Sullivan and Oberman built factories, careers and fortunes under the contract labor system, an equally youthful and energetic Kate Richards O'Hare was on a collision course with their success. On April 19, 1919, O'Hare began serving a five-year federal sentence at the Missouri penitentiary for an antiwar speech she had given in Bohman, North Dakota, some months earlier, a sentence that would change her life and contribute to reforms in inmate labor practices.

O'Hare exposed the harsh working conditions, verbal and physical abuse and cruel punishment for failing to meet unreasonable work quotas in her book *In Prison*, published by Alfred Knopf in 1923. She horrified the public with her description of the "black hole," a cell completely devoid of light and furnishings where inmates could be punished for falling short in their piecework. Rations consisted of a half teacup of water and two small squares of thin bread per day. Kate O'Hare's prison sentence was commuted by President Woodrow Wilson in May 1920. Later, she was given a full pardon by President Calvin Coolidge.

While O'Hare was incarcerated at MSP, another international activist shared the women's quarters there with her. Emma Goldman, known as "Red Emma," was serving one of her several imprisonments for charges ranging from inciting a riot to advocating the use of birth control to opposition to World War I. She was incredibly controversial. Teddy Roosevelt called her a "madwoman…a mental as well as a moral pervert." The *San Francisco Call* noted that she was a "despicable creature…[a] snake…unfit to live in a civilized country." The government called her the "ablest and most dangerous" anarchist in the country, and she was pursued much of her life by two of the most notorious law enforcement officials in American history, Anthony Comstock and J. Edgar Hoover. She is credited with having had tremendous influence on the founders of Planned Parenthood and the American Civil Liberties Union. She began publication of *Mother Earth* in 1906, a radical anarchist journal.

In the fall of 1953, a young Kansas City boy was kidnapped and brutally murdered. A week later, the murderers, Carl Austin Hall and Bonnie Heady, were arrested. They were tried and sentenced to death for their crimes. The federal government had no facilities to carry out the execution, so MSP was selected to carry out their sentence.

By 1954, the state penitentiary had gained a reputation for having the bloodiest forty-seven acres in America, as noted by *Time* magazine. The population grew to the point that six to eight inmates might be confined to a single cell. The prison was deteriorating and overcrowded, and a violent riot broke out on September 23. The event began in the maximum-security E Hall, which housed the more violent criminals. By the time order was restored, four inmates were dead and three guards and thirty prisoners were injured. Eight buildings were destroyed or damaged by fire. Two minor riots followed a month later, on October 23 and 24, resulting in the death of another inmate and the injury of thirty-six others.

By the 1960s, a series of assaults had made national headlines and brought attention to the prison. Between 1963 and 1964, there were 550 different accounts of assaults and hundreds of stabbings. A lack of administrative control from the warden was cited as the cause. E.V. Nash had been given the position after the riots of 1954 in the hope that he could restore order. This scandal brought about an administrative review and a report promoting the removal of Nash as warden. On December 18, 1964, Warden Nash took his own life in a house directly across from the state penitentiary with a gunshot to his head.

Missouri State Penitentiary, vintage postcard. *Courtesy Janice Tremeear.*

Within the grounds stands one small building isolated in a fenced courtyard. Between the years 1937 and 1989, thirty-nine or forty prisoners were put to death inside this tiny, ominous chamber. All but one of the executions used cyanide gas pumped into the sealed chamber. George "Tiny" Mercer was the first man executed in the state of Missouri, for the rape and murder of twenty-two-year-old Karen Keeten. There was a suspected leak in the chamber, and Tiny received a lethal injection on January 26, 1989. Mercer was the first execution after the 1977 reinstatement of capital punishment. Dan Terry, paranormal investigator and author of several books on ghost sightings conducted a dowsing rod question-and-answer session within the chamber. The session was filmed and recorded the rods answering in the affirmative when the spirits were asked if Mercer was present within the room. Dan presented a video of session at ParaCon 2011 held at the "haunted" Arlington Inn in DeSoto, Missouri.

After being decommissioned in October 2004, several plans were developed to begin demolition on the buildings. The more historical buildings were spared the fate of others in September 2007 when demolition took place on various locations within the complex. Reports of paranormal activity surfaced only after the destruction of buildings at the site. Reports, vague as they have been, include cell doors slamming on their own, apparitions and laughter ringing out in the buildings.

There are also rumors suggesting that the facility is a UFO base. Several photos have been circulated showing strange lights and shapes hovering above the facility. Jefferson City is not the only Missouri location with such reports. Lebanon, on I-44, has been another site with strange sightings. Springfield, Kansas City and Lake of the Ozarks have all had sightings. Montgomery County, where I spent the majority of my childhood, was notorious during my teenage years for UFO reports. A classmate and her boyfriend spoke of seeing one and being chased by it.

I watched unknown flying objects at sunset and after dark; they would remain completely still in the sky, with the entire object changing colors. The objects would move in quick motion, only to stop and hover and then fly upward, out of sight, at a forty-five-degree angle. Missouri contains more mysteries than simply the lingering dead.

Folks living next door to the prison in the 1940s reported that it was very eerie in the summer, with no air conditioning and the windows open, they could hear the prisoners in the hospital ward (which was on the west side, apparently) moaning and crying. Modern-day investigators list orbs, touching by unseen hands, photographs of eerie faces in long empty cells, laughing, cell doors slamming, creeping shadows, mists, cold spots, odd sounds and more as all being contained within the decaying structure that once was the site of gruesome deaths.

HAUNTED TAVERN

Generations of Jefferson City residents know the camaraderie and libations at the corner of 700 West Main Street. The tenth-oldest continually operating pub west of the Mississippi River, Paddy Malone's, has changed hands and names several times during its 140-year history. Other than during prohibition, its role as a neighborhood anchor is unchanged. Rumor has it that Cole County was the third-wettest county during the bootlegging days. Taverns were both gathering places and sources of local news. The three-story brick building on West Main Street in Jefferson City hasn't changed much in all those years.

Unsubstantiated rumors paint a colorful picture of the corner building housing a brothel upstairs in the early 1900s, an ongoing card game with Missouri's top officials through the mid-century decades and even Frank James's first drink as a free man after being pardoned by Governor Thomas Crittenden in 1882. An abstract records a building at the location in 1891. However, Sanborn Fire Insurance maps show a building having been on that lot since 1870. Records at the Cole County Historical Society suggest that a building on that corner was first erected in 1863 by Joseph Knaup as a blacksmith shop. The River Cliff subdivision—Bolivar to Clay Streets and Main Street to the river bluff—didn't see development until 1870, when the area became known as "Rich Man's Hill" because a well-to-do judge was the first to build in the area.

The building was constructed in 1863 originally to house a tack and saddle shop, but it morphed into the West End Saloon in 1870. The tavern then became the Bridge Exchange when the Bolivar Street Bridge was opened in 1896, but it was referred to as the "First Chance, Last Chance" in the vernacular, since Callaway County was a dry county and Cole was wet. In the 1970s, this architectural piece of community history was almost lost to the Urban Renewal Capitol West Project, but former owners were able to preserve it. It went on to become Pat's Place with new ownership in the 1940s, and it added the Irish flare in 1992. When a new owner took over in 2000, he changed the name to Paddy Malone's, drawing from his mother's heritage.

Rumors of doors closing and sounds of feet running over the floors were among the tales associated with the tavern. The spirits of the bar appear to be those of a positive nature, however, and when a Ouija board was brought onto the scene, the present-day owners began hearing from the spirits themselves.

One seems to be that of a thirteen-year-old boy who might have been running across the floor as he played with the owners' dogs. The spirit spelled the initials "FAZ" through the board, so that has become the name used when referring to the boy. A week later, another séance downstairs was conducted in the pub. A different spirit tried to finish spelling the boy's name. This spirit was Frederick Andrew, and the last name started with a Z. Yet another spirit was a prostitute from the early days, when the third floor was used as a brothel, and referred to herself as "bitch." There's also the "woman who worked upstairs," as the older townspeople call her.

Personal objects are discovered in places impossible for the owners' pets to have reached, a man's greasy handprints appear high on their apartment wall and water faucets turn on by themselves. But none of that compares to what one cleaning lady experienced. While working upstairs, the woman sensed that someone was behind her. She turned and saw nothing. Once she walked into the living room, though, she saw a man sitting on the couch wearing an old-time white shirt. She turned on her heels and left the room. So far, this is the only reported sighting of an apparition. Other employee accounts are more simple occurrences, such as doors slamming on their own.

Old Women's State Prison/Insane Asylum

C old spots are reported, doors are heard closing and the entity of an old lady wearing a gray uniform sitting at a table has been seen here at the old women's prison. However, there are no tables in the building. Orbs have been photographed and white mists observed on the site. The old prison has been abandoned quite possibly since 1990 and is notorious for hauntings among the locals. A group of people reportedly refuse to go back there after having had a terrifying experience at the jail. They claimed that you could hear voices whispering. It is said that if you go upstairs in the shop, footsteps will chase you out. The most horrifying claim made was that a soda can was observed sitting in the doorway of the prison when they saw a hand reach out from the shadows to grab it. The prison is tricky to locate and is said to be guarded by a man living nearby who reportedly shoots at anyone who tries to get near the building.

Brandi Ousley Tells of the Legends of Haunted Prisons

Brandi Ousley e-mailed me this account.

The old insane asylum, that was a prison for years that eventually got moved because of it getting flooded that now sits empty on 63/54 going toward Columbia. You can see it from the highway when you make that right hand loop getting off 63 toward Columbia, it's up the road a little bit, but it's on the left. I have friends who use to work at that prison, I'm not sure of the last time it was an active prison, But the activity that's in that building is unreal. drastic cold spots, an older woman in a grey uniform sitting at a table that isn't there, door's slamming, white mists, footsteps, chilling screams, low, but dark laughter, something shoving you, following you, my friend Marie, was on night watch, went to go get something out of one of the cells they were using as storage, got locked in the lights shut off and when she got the other guards attention had 3 giant scratches on her leg like something was trying to drag her, she said when you go to the wing that was the old shop you hear high pitched ringing like there was someone with a saw, and a lot of footsteps/running.

There are a couple of old bridges that are hard to find that are reported haunted but I'm not sure of the location, and one of the places is to be said to have a light that follow's you and then disappears when you get closer. One of the bridges, you shut your car off, and you roll down the hill, bloody footprints in the sand coming from the water that just stops, the bridges and all of this I've never been to, but eventually would like to...lol...let me know if any of this helps...I think the biggest thing I have the most interest in is the Prison... The "Alcatraz" of Missouri as Marie would put it...

Ever heard of "The Wall"? The prison there off of cherry street? Used to be called JCCC... it was the second highest lockdown in Missouri. They moved the prisoner's there, but that's the most deathly haunted places....an over 220+ year old building that used to be the mental hospital before they

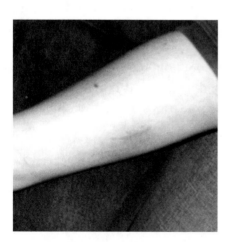

There are occasional reports of people being scratched by unseen entities at haunted locations. *Photo by Janice Tremeear.*

moved it to Fulton. By deathly haunted, that's exactly what it means...
I've been there, never toured it, but you get this dark, sense of dread
the closer and closer you get to it. Puts you on a different level within
yourself. It held Pretty Boy Floyd and James Earl Ray.

MEN IN BLACK

No one seems to know for sure who these individuals are. Reports say that the men in black have been seen standing next to people in places as mundane as the Target store in Jefferson City, Missouri, or walking briskly as if on a mission and dressed in an older business suit and wearing sunglasses. They are heard to mumble to themselves in something not quite English and yet not another language either. Their voices are deep and odd, wrong to our ears, and items they've been seen purchasing are equally strange, ladies' diapers, for instance.

These same types of men were witnessed weeks later at Lake of the Ozarks, Missouri, about forty-five miles away from Jefferson City. They displayed the same deep voice as the one seen in Target at Jefferson City. Apparently, these men all possess the same manner of walking strangely, as if their joints don't work quite correctly. Always alone and wearing sunglasses, they attempt to blend in with the tourists. They are seen on days when a bad event happens in the area. One such incident was when a boat blew up on the lake, and shortly afterward, two of the strange men were seen in a nearby hotel. They give off a feeling of malevolence about them according to reports of witnesses, much as some of the shadow beings do. Another boating accident resulted in the death of a young girl, and again one of these men in black appeared in the vicinity. Hotel customers have reported these strange men late at night wearing sunglasses.

Another strange man was sighted in Jefferson City on another occasion. Thin, mechanical and mumbling to the point of buzzing, he appeared to stalk the witness throughout the store. Since those encounters, different men, bearing the same robotic, soulless mannerisms, have appeared at the Lake of the Ozarks. They were a little thinner but also wore sunglasses and appeared to be between forty-five and fifty-five. They often wore layers and layers of clothing. Perhaps they are of the category of beings called "Watchers," merely observing events rather than participating in them.

DARK HOLLOW ROAD

There's a Callaway County road that evil creatures roam at night, according to some people. The legend of Dark Hollow Road has been passed down from generation to generation.

The sign says County Road 409, but those who know the stories of this doomed drive call it Dark Hollow Road. Most inhabitants near the road know the story of a black panther that escaped from a traveling circus near Mokane during the 1940s. Storytellers said that the ghost of the panther stalks the woods along Dark Hollow Road at night in search of unsuspecting victims.

A man rode his motorcycle through there years ago. His motorcycle was later found, along with one of his boots (and his leg still in it). The rest of the remains were never located. The panther or the creature of Dark Hollow got him and took care of him—so goes the reasoning of some of the locals in the area. People around Callaway County are pretty familiar with the stories of the panther, but the woods along Dark Hollow have a lot more stories to tell, such as the story of the drunken teenage couple who died in a car crash on the road years ago. They say if you turn headlights on and off, a set of ghost headlights will appear in front of you. The ghost headlights then pass through your car, leaving every passenger covered in blood. Other stories tell of unexplained screams in the night. Dozens of horror stories are associated with this seven-mile stretch of dirt and gravel between Fulton and a small cemetery in Hams Prairie. Some claims suggest that the graves there glow at night, as restless spirits try to contact the living. "If you go through there on Halloween, I'd say, be careful" is a common refrain. Folks are cautioned "never travel alone on Dark Hollow Road, especially at night. There's screaming and hollers there, always screaming."

NEARBY GHOSTS

A ghost is someone who hasn't made it—in other words, who died, and they don't know they're dead. So they keep walking around and thinking that you're inhabiting their…let's say, their domain. So they're aggravated with you.
—*Sylvia Browne*

COLUMBIA

Columbia is the fifth-largest city in Missouri. Columbia was settled in pre-Columbian times by the mound-building Mississippian culture of Native Americans. When European explorers arrived, the area was populated by the Osage and Missouri Indians. In 1678, La Salle claimed all of Missouri for France. In 1818, a group of settlers incorporated under the Smithton Land Company purchased more than two thousand acres and established the village of Smithton near present-day downtown Columbia. In 1821, the settlers moved and renamed the settlement Columbia. Columbia's later infrastructure was wholly untouched by the Civil War.

The Missouri Theater in Columbia is haunted by the ghost of the former owner, who makes clanking noises, and the curtains have been known to rise and fall without prompting.

The Conley House in Columbia was built in 1868–69 as a private residence, and the house is now owned by the University of Missouri. According to Conley descendants, the house is haunted by the ghost of Aunt Sally Conley. Known to have been a disagreeable woman, Aunt Sally requested to be buried in the north wall of the Conley House when she died. Rumor says that her final resting place is in the fireplace of the house. She haunts the residence at night, but only when the attic door is left ajar.

COLUMBIA COLLEGE

When this college was originally founded in 1851, it was an all-female school called Christian College. One young student was engaged to a Confederate soldier and vowed to wear only gray clothing so long as

Civil War weapons at reenactment; some are replicas and others are vintage guns used in battle, Springfield, Missouri. *Photo by Dean Pestana.*

he did—at least until it could be replaced by a white wedding gown. However, her fiancé was killed by Union soldiers not far from the college, and the girl jumped from a three-story building called the Conservatory, now known as Williams Hall. The "Gray Lady" is seemingly benevolent. She is glimpsed as a fleeting figure in gray, passing through buildings and creating an almost indescribable presence. At other times, she is said to do small favors for students, such as opening windows on hot days, at times evening completing their ironing.

THE RESIDENCE ON FRANCIS QUADRANGLE

Francis Quadrangle reflects the rich history of the University of Missouri. Built in 1867, the Residence is the cornerstone of the eighteen red brick buildings that compose the quadrangle's nationally recognized historic district and has hosted many national and international figures. In 1902, Mark Twain dined there while on campus to receive an honorary degree. President Harry S Truman stayed in the Residence during a visit in 1950, and Eleanor Roosevelt rested and changed for dinner in an upstairs bedroom in 1959.

The Residence is built on the site of an earlier house completed in 1843. During the Civil War, three hundred Union soldiers occupied the campus. Their commanding officer, Colonel Merrill, resided in the Residence but not for long. On November 28, 1865, the Residence was destroyed by fire. Following the fire, the Missouri legislature appropriated $10,000 for a new Residence and other improvements, marking the first state appropriation to the university. In 1867, the $8,000 home was completed, and President Daniel Read and his family took up residence.

In May 1874, President Read's wife, Alice, died in the Residence. Her death, coupled with a report in an April 1890 edition of the *Columbia Missouri Herald* that "ghostly apparitions" were seen dancing in the windows of the upstairs bedrooms, fueled rumors that the house is haunted. Reports of ghosts still circulate today.

GHOSTS OF FAYETTE AT
CENTRAL METHODIST UNIVERSITY

Fayette is a beautiful town located thirteen miles from Boonville and twenty-six miles from Columbia, settled in the rolling farmland of central Missouri. Benjamin Cooper made the county's first permanent settlement in 1810. Two years later, Cooper had one of several defensive forts against the Indians in the War of 1812. Iowa, Sauk and Fox tribes ceded their claims to this area in 1824.

Settled largely by southerners, Howard County and Fayette lie in Missouri's Little Dixie region. The Battle of Fayette was fought on land where the university now sits. The battle occurred on September 24,

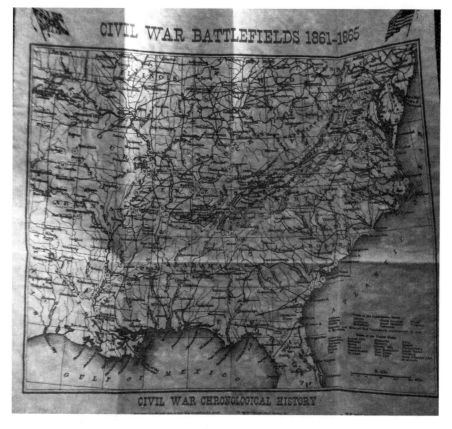

Civil War battlefield map. *Courtesy Janice Tremeear.*

1864, when two bands of guerrillas (Southern sympathizers) assaulted a fortified Union garrison in Fayette. It was not until after the coming of the Missouri/Kansas/Texas Railroad in 1873 that the town enjoyed renewed growth.

Howard Payne Hall

This coed dorm was originally Howard Payne Female College in the late 1800s. Howard Payne Hall, or HP for the students attending Central Methodist University (CMU), is the most haunted spot on campus. In the wintertime around Christmas, it has been reported that late at night, you can see a young lady standing outside the dorm. Although her name is unknown, the story goes that one night in the early 1900s, she was returning to her dorm from a long night of studying at the library. As she was walking around the corner of the building toward the entrance, some bricks came loose from the second-story wall and fell on her head, killing her.

In the 1930s, it was said that a young man was on the third floor of HP drinking heavily with some friends. When he was told that his frat brothers had found out that he was drinking, he knew that he would be punished and likely kicked out of the frat. Highly intoxicated, he made the wrong choice of jumping out the open window. He now haunts the north wing on the first floor.

The fifth floor of Howard Payne is the most well known. It's so haunted that the school has actually securely locked the floor off from students. Spring finals in the 1940s; saw a young woman about to graduate with a degree in music. The week before finals, she hanged herself in her dorm room; no one knows why. In the week before spring finals late at night, you can hear her practicing her cello. The only people allowed on the fifth floor now are resident assistants. Many of the RAs have said that in the room where this girl killed herself, the door is often found unlocked, lights on, the water running and the fan on; many strange noises are heard coming from the room. One RA reported that as he was leaving the room, he turned off the lights. As he looked in the room one last time, he saw the girl hanging from one of the pipes, and blood was dripping down the walls. The second he flipped the lights back on, the girl and the blood were gone.

The Stacks

Located in the Smiley Library on campus, it is believed that there is a serial killer trapped in the old archive area of the library known by students as the Stacks. It's said that back in the 1860s, while the school was being rebuilt (due to the Civil War), a black man was running from the authorities who were looking to execute him for the crimes of multiple rapes and murders. He stopped in Fayette to help rebuild the library to make some money before continuing his escape. But while he was in the Stacks repairing a wall, the wall fell on him, crushing him. The man in the Stacks is seen and/or felt by female students primarily.

Brannock Hall

During the Civil War, CMU was occupied by the Confederate army. Almost every building has a Civil War story, but none as sad as Brannock Hall. Now used as the admissions office, during the war it was used as a stable for generals' horses. A small boy who was a resident of Fayette took care of the stable and the horses. One night, while the boy was there late, the stable mysteriously caught fire, killing all of the horses and the little boy. It's been reported that you can hear the horses, and sometimes you'll see the little boy running around trying to get his chores done.

Givens Hall

Givens Hall was built on campus as a place of lodging for people visiting the college. Built at the end of the 1800s, it is still used as a guesthouse. Many of the old original pictures and pieces of furniture are still in the house. Although no one is completely sure about any deaths taking place in the house, there have been numerous accounts of people hearing strange sounds at night, the sinks turning on when no one is in the bathroom and voices of adults and children. Each room in the house has its own story.

Spook Hollow Light, Booneville

Northwest of Jefferson City lies Booneville, near the banks of the Missouri River in Cooper County. Booneville is the county seat of Cooper County. The city was the site of a skirmish early in the Civil War on July 17, 1861. Union forces defeated a small and poorly equipped force of the Missouri State Guard in the first Battle of Boonville. As in the case of most hauntings, tragedy could very well play in role in ghostly visits.

The tale of Spook Hollow begins with a man by the name of Story who built a cabin of rough-hewn timbers with a "dog-run" or "turkey-trot" between the two rooms. He was a mystery to all who knew him, shunning public contact and keeping to himself. One day, a neighbor happened by, and Story's cabin was deserted, the ashes cold in the fireplace. Half-starved dogs were battling over scraps of food. His gun was left behind. As in the notions of the day, people assumed that he may have been murdered, or since he was not a "Christian man," he may have sold his soul to the devil and disappeared. His property was sold, and then the "Spook," already well-established after Story's disappearance, showed itself once a new family named Houston moved into the home in the spring of 1882. It was described as a dazzling ball of white light, with no variation in size and seemingly unaffected by climate. It skimmed the tree tops or hovered thirty inches above the ground, always showing up at the northern rim of the valley. Its speed was sometimes like a steady walk, or rushing along at twenty miles an hour. It always made a slow tour of the Story cabin after coming down the valley and paused at the four corners of the home before taking off out of the valley.

Dogs would run at the apparition barking and then halt and become terrified of it, whining, hiding beneath the cabin and howling as the light would hover at the gate. The bright light gave off no heat, and a V-shaped shadow loomed behind it that no light could penetrate. Voices of a man and boy arguing were heard to emanate from within the sphere, and sometimes two buckskin-clad legs appeared beneath the shadow.

The Spook apparently enjoyed coon hunting and stirred dogs into the hunt with an audible "HEEEEE-eeeee" coming from it. After the dogs treed a raccoon, the sounds of an axe felling the tree could be heard, followed by total silence. No sound of the kill and no trace of a fallen tree could be located. One October night, the Spook set a burr tree ablaze, but the fire died just as quickly, leaving the dried leaves and tree untouched.

The Spook was seen herding one hundred hogs through the woods with the sounds of "Shoey" and "Hee" pouring from within the bright globe. The Spook would often halt in the middle of roads, not allowing people on foot to pass, or would hover there and frighten the horses of travelers.

Years have passed with no further sightings of the Spook. Perhaps the ball of light left this realm as quietly and mysteriously at it arrived. Perhaps Mr. Story has moved on elsewhere.

GHOSTLY CARRIAGE

The late Bob Dyer not only researched the wild child "Boogie Man Bill" and Guinea Sam, but he also wrote songs collected from data provided by Charles van Ravensway, from whom the Spook Hollow story came via interviews of several citizens in the area of the events. This next tale had some basis in fact. It seems that an elderly couple once lived in a crumbling mansion on the bluff overshadowing the settlement of Overton Landing by the Missouri River near Booneville. They had apparently obtained a great fortune via the murder of a stranger who took refuge with them. The man had been carrying enough money to fulfill their wildest dreams; hers was obtaining a fine black silk dress and his the purchase of the finest carriage.

However, soon after this, the wife died and was buried in her fine yet ill-gotten silk dress. Her widow was now wealthy and soon remarried. Dyer's song carries the lyrics, "There came a phantom black carriage and a woman in a black silk gown," and as the newly married young wife watched, "The man got in and the carriage disappeared. It's been a long time now since it happened. There's nothing left now of the house on the bluff or the town. But people still see the carriage and a woman in a black silk gown."

The mansion is thought to still be standing near Woolridge, abandoned, and it may have been the ancestral home of the woman who originally told the story. It is a home with "a distinctly haunted quality about it," as Dyer said. Bob was employed as "riverlorian" for the Delta Queen Steamboat Company from 1999 until 2002. He wrote several books, was a poet and called himself a "songteller" with many albums.

ARROW ROCK

For generations, the Arrow Rock Bluff was a significant landmark on the Missouri River for Native Americans, explorers and early westward travelers. This flint-bearing, high limestone bluff first appeared on a 1732 French map as "Pierre a Fleche," literally translated as "Rock of Arrows." Archaeological evidence shows that for nearly twelve thousand years indigenous cultures used the Arrow Rock Bluff as a manufacturing site for flint tools and weapons.

After the War of 1812 and the subsequent peace treaties with Indians in 1815, large numbers of migrants from Kentucky, Tennessee and Virginia poured into the fertile Boone's Lick Country, so named for the salt spring, or "lick," across the river.

During the 1820s, travelers on what became the Santa Fe Trail crossed the river on the Arrow Rock ferry and filled their water barrels with fresh water at the "Big Spring" before heading west. In 1829, the town of Arrow Rock was founded on the bluff above the ferry crossing. Originally named Philadelphia, the town's name was changed in 1833 to coincide with the better-known landmark name, Arrow Rock.

Fires have beset Arrow Rock throughout its history. In August 1864, sparks from the stacks of steamboat *Isabella* set fire to the riverfront of Arrow Rock, and the flames destroyed four warehouses. On December 28, 1872, the most destructive fire ever known in central Missouri tore through the village. The fire originated in the upper room of John Gilpin's saloon, which was located on the corner of Fourth and Main Streets at the site of the present-day Arrow Rock Country Store. The January 22, 1873 edition of the *Saline County Progress* reported:

> *Monday night was a terrible night to the people of Arrow Rock. As evening came the shades gathered thick and black around us, and the cold searing wind from the north increased with each succeeding hour of darkness until the window panes chattered, the key-holes moaned and while interminable gales swept through the street and over the houses…As midnight came the town was hushed in slumber, the daylight perceivable being that in the office of Dr. Hurt. The doctor saw the reflection of a kindling upon the house immediately east of the Post Office.*

Two-story business buildings sprang up along the main street of this important river port during the 1850s. On July 11, 1901, a lamp ignited a fire in a two-story brick building and robbed the town of more than a dozen businesses, offices and residences.

The entire village of Arrow Rock has been designated a National Historic Landmark, recognizing its association with westward expansion, the Santa Fe Trail and artist George Caleb Bingham.

Arrow Rock Lyceum Theater

During the 1960s, Dr. and Mrs. John Lawrence, along with Mr. and Mrs. "Red" Argubright, co-owned the old Arrow Rock Baptist Church, left vacant when congregations consolidated due to a declining population in the village. The Lawrences and the Argubrights offered to convert the empty building to a theater. Mr. Henry Swanson, a professor at Christian College in Columbia, Missouri, now Columbia College, was engaged as artistic director and proposed the newly named Henry Swanson Hall's first budget at $3,500. The first season consisted of three nineteenth-century plays, opening with *The Importance of Being Earnest.*

In 1972, the Henry Swanson Hall (later known as the Lyceum) was built to house the twenty to twenty-five seasonal company members. The rustic-style dormitory included twelve air-conditioned double rooms and a basement that provided both storage and a rehearsal hall.

The end of the 1970s also made for the end of an era at the Lyceum. In 1979, Henry Swanson retired from the theater, and the board of directors began searching for a new artistic director to lead the theater into the next decade. In the 1980s, a young man named Michael Bollinger was hired by the Lyceum, where he served as AD for twenty-five years. During Mr. Bollinger's tenure, he expanded the Lyceum's reach by introducing twentieth-century musicals to the repertoire. In 1984, he produced a new musical about President Harry Truman called *The Buck Stops Here*, later performed at the Smithsonian Museum in Washington, D.C. The interest in the Lyceum was so great that it was becoming evident that the walls would have to expand to accommodate the growing audience and concessions; it was assured that the new building would preserve the quaintness of the converted nineteenth-century Baptist church.

In 2004, the Lyceum dormitory burned beyond repair. Thanks to the generosity of the Arrow Rock community, the company was housed in local bed-and-breakfasts, rental houses and private homes for the next three seasons while plans were finalized for a more permanent solution. These are the facts, and now comes the haunting—as always, passed along in the retelling of the tale. The stories that came about are believed to be connected to another fire in the theater.

A refurbishing in one of the dressing rooms was in progress at the time because of a previous fire. One of the actors reported hearing screaming as if coming from an eight-year-old girl. Upon asking one of the stagehands about it, the young actor was told that in 1994 some little girl had gotten trapped in the dressing room in a fire and haunted the theater now. The actor continued to witness odd occurrences, including looking up into the rafters to see a little girl watching the actors below. The sound of a little girl singing could be heard, yet something about it didn't seem right.

Then props disappeared just as they were needed onstage, and costumes were discovered ripped and stained. One night, a set piece almost crushed one of the main actresses. During another evening, the power went out, and in the blackness, the singing was heard as the theater became extremely cold. Breathing was also heard, as well as a child's giggle. Apparently, the girl's death resulted from a costume rack that jammed a door, with one of the actors mysteriously leaving the night of the accident. The girl is thought to be Carolyn Brown, who died in a fire suspected to have been set by an arsonist. Or so the tale of the Lyceum Theater goes.

THE CENTRALIA MASSACRE

The city of Centralia lies to the north of Jefferson City and became the site for one of the most brutal mass slayings of the Civil War.

On September 27, 1864, 22 unarmed Union soldiers returning home on leave were pulled from a train in Centralia and executed by Confederate bushwhackers under William T. "Bloody Bill" Anderson. A Union force pursuing the guerrillas was ambushed, and about 150 were killed; some were executed, and some were tortured first. Many of the bodies were mutilated and then stuffed with the remains of rotting cattle bones. The incident came to be known as the Centralia Massacre.

On that day, September 27, Jesse and Frank James rode into Centralia with a party of eighty guerrillas led by Anderson. In short order, they set about plundering the pro-Union town—breaking into homes, demanding money and helping themselves to food and whiskey—until a train entered the railroad station. Inside were 22 Union soldiers returning to their homes in Missouri and Iowa, on furlough after participating in General William Tecumseh Sherman's campaign through Tennessee and Georgia. They were unarmed. In short order, by Anderson's command, they were executed in cold blood.

A battalion of the Thirty-ninth Missouri Infantry entered Centralia not long after the murders and took up pursuit. South of town,

"Bloody Bill" Anderson, vintage postcard. *Courtesy Janice Tremeear.*

Anderson's guerrillas got word of the approaching force and set up an ambush. Being no match for the veteran guerrillas, the green volunteers were annihilated. That evening, Anderson's crew mutilated the bodies of the Union dead. Today, it's easy to miss that battlefield, marked only by a small bronze plaque on a dirt road. It is a quiet and serene patch of ground, the blood of that day having long become part of the soil, the grass growing and the seeds of the cottonwoods spinning together along the roadside.

Historian T.J. Stiles's illuminating biography *Jesse James: Last Rebel of the Civil War* paints the legend differently, and the true face of the killer fills the foreground. Stiles's reassessment casts James as a political terrorist, one whose bank and train robberies were performed as political acts promoting the cause of the vanquished Confederacy and the removal of Federal occupation forces from the former slave states. Jesse James set out to shake up the country. The Confederate guerrilla turned bank robber selected banks controlled by Republican leaders. His men wore Klan hoods as they held up trains. A slave owner, he and his family kept their servants in perpetual bondage long after the Civil War. Jesse's goal was to redirect Missouri and the nation toward extremism, and he partially succeeded. Reconstruction was abandoned and, with it, the cause for civil rights. Decades of segregation, racial discrimination and lynching were aided by James's political legacy.

Jesse James began his terrorist education as a member of Anderson's "death squads," as Stiles labeled the Missouri bushwhackers. He described the aftermath of the Centralia Massacre:

> *The rebels walked among the dead, crushing faces with rifle butts and shoving bayonets through the bodies, pinning them to the ground. Frank James bent down to loot one of the corpses, pulling free a sturdy leather belt. Others slid knives out of their sheaths and knelt down to work. One by one, they cut 17 scalps loose, carefully tied them to their saddles and bridles. At least one guerrilla carved the nose off a victim. Others sliced off ears—or sawed off heads and switched their bodies. Someone pulled the trousers off one corpse, cut off the penis and shoved it in the dead man's mouth…In this blood-drunk crew, of course, stood Jesse James.*

The spirits of the Union soldiers massacred at the local train station are often seen roaming the local business district, cursing the James brothers and "Bloody Bill" Anderson for their whiskey-induced southern

Left: Jesse James, vintage postcard. *Courtesy Janice Tremeear.*

Below: Type of cannon used during Civil War, from a reenactment held in Springfield, Missouri. *Photo by Dean Pestana.*

aristocracy blood drenching that accounted for nearly two hundred souls' early demise in a turkey shoot in which affluent southerners well-heeled in literacy and presidential connections masqueraded as Robin Hoods but really were well-financed criminal fronts.

One witness reported experiencing bloodcurdling screams, shadow entities and children observed laughing and playing. Rumors say that most of the town is haunted by the events of the massacre.

BIBLIOGRAPHY

Dyer, Bob. *Songteller*. This compact disc, released in 1991, contains nineteen songs by Bob Dyer originally released on two cassette tapes (the tapes are no longer available) entitled *River of the Big Canoes* and *Treasure in the River*. Big Canoe Records, 513 High Street, Boonville, Missouri. The songs "The Phantom Black Carriage," "The Wild Child of Gooch's Mill" and "Guinea Sam" provided insights into those tales.

Gilbert, Joan. *Missouri Ghosts*. Hallsville, MO: Mohgo Books, 2001.

Henry, Michael. *Ghosts of St. Charles*. Charleston, SC: The History Press, 2010.

Mott, A.S. *Ghost Stories of Missouri: True Tales of Ghostly Hauntings*. N.p.: Ghost House Books, 2006. Originally printed Auburn, WA: Lone Pine Publishing, 1808.

Offutt, Jason. *Darkness Walks: The Shadow People Among Us*. Charlottesville, VA: Anomalist Books, 2009.

———. *Haunted Missouri: A Ghostly Guide to the Show-Me-State's Most Spirited Spots*. Kirksville, MO: Truman State University Press, 2007.

————. *Paranormal Missouri, Show Me Your Monsters.* Atglen, PA: Schiffer Publishing, 2010.

Prosser, Lee. *Missouri Hauntings.* Atglen, PA: Schiffer Publishing, 2008.

Scott, Beth and Michale Norman. *Haunted Heartland.* New York: Warner Books, 1985.

Tremeear, Janice. *Haunted Ozarks.* Charleston, SC: The History Press, 2011.

————. *Missouri's Haunted Route 66: Ghosts Along the Mother Road.* Charleston, SC: The History Press, 2010.

————. *Wicked St. Louis.* Charleston, SC: The History Press, 2011.

Van Ravenswaay, Charles. "Spook Hollow." Written October 25, 1941, and submitted to Western Historical Manuscript Collection, University of Missouri–Columbia, Columbia, Missouri, 1985.

ABOUT THE AUTHOR

Courtesy Charlene Wells

Janice has written three other books for The History Press: *Missouri's Haunted Route 66: Ghosts Along the Mother Road*; *Haunted Ozarks*; and *Wicked St. Louis*. She has worked with paranormal teams and founded two, training members how to conduct investigations. Interested in all things paranormal from a young age, Janice now works independently, joining other groups as a guest investigator. She also teaches the use of dowsing rods in paranormal investigating at conventions and events such as Pagan Pride Day in Springfield, Missouri.

Janice has given lectures across Missouri on the paranormal and on the historical significance of haunted locations in the state. She has appeared on the *Itchy Show*, an independent program aired out of St. Louis, Missouri; Westplex 107 from St. Louis; and KSPR radio in Springfield, Missouri. She's also been interviewed on KSP33 TV and been featured in both news and magazine articles.

She was the first paranormal author to speak at VisionCon 2011 and VisionCon 2012. She was one of the headlining presenters at ParaCon 2011 and a speaker at the twentieth anniversary of the St. Louis Pagan Picnic in 2012. She also teaches a class called Organic Belly Dance and has her own performing Tribal-style belly dance troupe, Ragdoll Brigade. She is an energy body worker and is currently attending school to become a licensed massage therapist (LMT). She is busy not only plotting her first fiction novel but also continuing to research the paranormal and work on books for The History Press.